The Mystery of the Kingdom through Dreams, Visions and the Word

Kingdom Economic

For it is for you to know the mystery of the Kingdom: Mark 4:11- "And he said unto them, unto you it is given to know the mystery (secret) of the kingdom of God: but unto them that are without, all these things are done in parables." (KJV)

By: Ms. Deborah Caldwell

Copyright @2021 by Deborah Caldwell

All rights reserved. No part of this book may be reproduced in any form or by any electronic or mechanical means, including information storage and retrieval systems, without permission in writing from the publisher, except by reviewers, who may quote brief passages in a review.

This publication contains the opinions and ideas of its author. It is intended to provide helpful and informative material on the subjects addressed in the publication. The author and publisher specifically disclaim all responsibility for any liability, loss or risk, personal or otherwise, which is incurred as a consequence, directly or indirectly, of the use and application of any of the contents of this book.

WORKBOOK PRESS LLC
187 E Warm Springs Rd,
Suite B285, Las Vegas, NV 89119, USA

Website: https://workbookpress.com/
Hotline: 1-888-818-4856
Email: admin@workbookpress.com

Ordering Information:
Quantity sales. Special discounts are available on quantity purchases by corporations, associations, and others. For details, contact the publisher at the address above.

ISBN-13: 978-1-956017-77-9 (Paperback Version)
978-1-956017-78-6 (Digital Version)

REV. DATE: 23.11.2021

Acknowledgements

My deepest appreciation to my mother, Vernal Drew who believed in me she always pushes me to become the best I am to be. Mom, you are my inspiration a wonderful mother and friend.

To my beautiful children my son Adrian, also my oldest and only boy you have taught me to handle my struggles.

To my oldest daughter, your heart and zeal for your mom and others has inspired me to not give up.

To Roshonda, your determination, creativity, diverse potential encourages me to explore my identity and potential.

To Crystal, you a noted for your strong character as a special child have impacted my life in many so many ways.

To Sophia, your tenderness of heart and determination and zeal for righteousness is commendable.

To my Heavenly Father and creator, who was patient with me and through Love and Kindness drew me into your kingdom all the Glory belongs to you. Thank you for direction and guidance all that you have taught to become a woman of purpose. I am eternally grateful. Amen

Preface

Deborah Caldwell have experience a life changing of the heart through the Mystery of the Kingdom through Dream, Vision, and the Word of God she has experience dreams and from them she has learn how to interpret the dreams that a given by God through his Holy Spirit.

In this book Deborah will talk about the dreams and visions from scriptures in the bible these dreams if understood and interpreted correctly can be applied to our life and lived out.

Deborah will not talk about the interpretation of dream this book will come separately so you can separate and understand how to interpret your dreams without being confused. Jesus talked a lot about the kingdom of Heaven it is a Mystery, but to those who seek shall be satisfied. Come with me as we discover the Mystery of the kingdom through dreams, visions and the Word of God.

Introduction

Some of you reading this book may find your lives a mystery-Jesus talked a lot about The Mystery of the Kingdom. Our lives seem a mystery at times. We should learn why we are here and the purpose for our lives. God is want you to know the mystery and the interpretations of your dreams, he speaks to us through dreams and visions. This book is a record of my personal encounter as well biblical events from the word of God. As you read this book I pray that you grasp an understanding of what it is to have dreams and visions which is another way God speaks to his people.

I have written a separated book on the interpretation of Dreams, so this will be separate in order for you to understand the dreams and how they are to be interpreting. God do not deal with us through fortune telling, zodiac, divination, horoscopes, hypnotisms, charmers, passive mind state. Gods' method of dealing with us is always through our hearts or spirit for God is a spirit being.

Magic – sorcery – "black" or "white".

Black magic produces evil results through such methods as curses, spells destruction of models of one's enemy and alliance with evil Spirits often takes the form of witchcraft, white magic tries to undo curses or spells, and to use occult forces for the good of—others. This is not a book about all of the demonic forces. We will cover this in my book exposing false prophets, teachers, doctrines. This is just a brief exposure to the dark side. God is light in him is no darkness. This book is based on the mystery of the kingdom.

This non-fiction book explores dreams, visions, and

the Word of God, as exemplified among people and events in the Bible, and what God may be saying concerning the mysteries of his Kingdom. The author and writer also included her own dreams from God and how God revealed to her his purpose for her life through Dream and Visions.

Deborah gives examples from the Bible of real people trusting God when faced with uncertain conditions and situations. The example of Abraham, King David, Solomon and others, will demonstrate this faith in God to readers more vibrantly and in relatable terms. Giving examples of God speaking to people through dreams and vision what these dreams can reveal about the potential path.

Dreams will help assist readers in writing down their dreams and asking God to speak and reveal his message that he speaks about one's life. Deborah Caldwell comes from the Ministry of Jesus Christ Holiness Church founder and owner Bishop Jimmy Boles and Nettie Boles of Shreveport, Louisiana where she serves in the Ministry from 2003-2013. Deborah was ordained and Licensed as a Minister under Bishop Jimmy and Nettie Boles, but Deborah was called and ordained by God when she was in her mothers' womb.

God visit her in Dreams and Visions, while Deborah began to study and Teach Gods' word she begins to see a revelation of Dreams and Visions in the bible with Gods' Prophets, as she continues to have these dreams and vision she begin to see that God has always visits his people through this gift. Deborah did not know how to interpret her dreams or know what they meant, in 2013 God begin to teach her how to interpret her dreams as she studies his word.

God being to give revelations of his Word where people in the bible had dreams for God was speaking while it was quiet and peaceful. Joseph had a dream that dream can into reality. Joseph also interprets his dream, and the bakers dream, and Pharaoh's see Genesis 41:1-36. Deborah belongs to a group with over 50,000 members that help those who join or just visit on face book. You too can learn what God is speaking to you through dreams, visions and the Word.

Table of Contents

Dedication XII
Acknowledgement V
Preface VII
Introduction IX
Where It All Begins 15
Go to Moriah 17
An Open Heaven 20
A Place of Offering 26
The Prophetic Anointing of a Prophet 30
A Deeper Walk 33
David Charge to Solomon 39
Overshadow Me 44
Understanding the Prophetic 48
Standing in the Gap: Intercessory Prayer 51
Power of the Cross 58
The Mantle 63
To Live A Godly Life 81
The Word of God 89
The Time of Pruning 101
The Wind 110
Prophecy and Dreams Interpretation 121

DEDICATION

This book is dedicated to the Lord Jesus Christ, the Lamb who shed his blood for all mankind. His sacrifice at the cross has provided freedom for all and I am forever grateful for his love and patient toward all who believe and trust in him... To our Lord and King is the Glory.

Chapter 1

Where It All Begin

"Bring joy to your servant, O Lord"
(Psalm 86:4a).

And Abraham said of Sarah his wife, she is my sister and Abimelech king of Gerar sent, and took Sarah.

Genesis 20:2 (KJV)

2 God came to Abimelech, in a dream by night, and said to him, behold thou art but a dead man for the woman which thou hast taken for she is a man wife.

 Abraham, feared for his life does this mean Abraham did not trust God? Abraham was a man of faith pronounce as the father of many nations regardless of his faith Abraham, was still a man who had not been perfected in his walk with God the walk of progressive sanctification.

In A Dream

Genesis 20: 6-7

6 And God said unto him a dream, Yea I know that thou didst this in the integrity of thy heart; for I also withheld thee from sinning against me: therefore, suffered I thee not to touch her.

7 Now therefore restore the man his wife; for he is a prophet, and he shall pray for thee, and thou shall live: and if thou restore her not, know thou that thou shall surely die, thou, and all that are thine.

God paid (called) Abraham, a prophet we know that one of the access of a prophet is to pray (intercede) on behalf of someone else.

Chapter 2
Go to Moriah

God tells Abraham, to go to Moriah take his only son Isaac to be sacrificed. Moriah in the Hebrew word means mound or hill; there are churches that are called Mount Moriah in this day and time.

Genesis 22:2 (KJV)

2 And he said, Take now thy son, thine only son Isaac, whom thou loves, and get thee into the land of Moriah; and offer him there for a burnt offering upon one of the mountains which I will tell thee of.

So Abraham obeyed and did exactly what God told him to do well God gives the best instruction if we would only listen to him he will lead us and guide in every aspect in our lives.

John 3:16 (KJV)

16 For God so loved the world that he gave his only begotten son that whosoever believeth in him should not perish, but have everlasting life. This is a picture of the son of God sacrifice on the cross at Calvary.

1 John 4:9 (KJV)

9 In this was manifested the love of God toward us, because that God sent his only begotten son into the world, that we might live through him.

The Burnt Offering

Not only did Abraham operate in the office of a prophet (intercessor), but he also operates in the office of the priest when he brought his only son to Moriah he prepared for a burnt offering.

Leviticus 1:3 (KJV)

3 If his offering be a burnt sacrifice of the herd, let him offer a male without blemish: he shall offer it of his own voluntary will at the door of the tabernacle of the congregation before the Lord.

God gave Moses instruction on how the priest was to operate in the congregation of his ordered pattern the burnt offering of sacrifice unto God On the cross Christ was our burnt offering.

Ephesians 5:2 (KJV)

2 And walk in love, as Christ also hath loved us, and hath given himself for us an offering and a sacrifice to God for a sweet smelling savior.

The Obedience of One Man

Because of the obedience of Abraham we have the same blessings of Abraham, we are called to operate as prophets and priest a royal priest hood a holy nation as prophets. God visit in dreams and vision as well as his word we are heir's joint heirs with Jesus Christ. He did so that he could life through us and we can be obedient to God through him.

Genesis 22:13-14 (KJV)

13 And Abraham lifted up his eyes, and looked, and behold behind him a ram caught in a thicket by his horns: and

Abraham went and took the ram, and offered him up for a burnt offering in the stead of his son.

14 And Abraham called the name of that place Jehovah-Jireh: as it is said to this day, in the mount of the Lord it shall be seen.

(Jehovah Jireh) the Lord will provide.

Chapter 3

An Open Heaven

I can remember the first time I heard this term open heaven I was busy in my house just relocated from one state to another. I was up early around 5:30 a.m. every morning praying. On a particular day I was awake cleaning all of a suddenly I heard in my spirit an open Heaven. I was not aware that I was under an open Heaven, but I was aware that Gods presence was with me all day long. Sometime I would just sit and rest I could feel his presence in the room and tears would just fall down my face and I would say I know you are here I feel your presence. It was such a peace in that place I begin to search the scriptures and here us where I found that the heaven really opens to us it is one of the blessings of Abraham, from generation to generation.

Prophetic Dreams

Genesis 28:12-13 (KJV)

12 And he dreamed, and beholds a ladder set up on the earth, and the top of it reached to heaven: and behold the angels of God ascending and descending on it.

13 And, behold, the Lord stood above it, and said, I am the Lord God of Abraham thy father, and the God of Isaac: the land whereon thou lies', to thee will I give it, and to thy seed;

I believe from that time forth Jacob, which is Abraham, grandson begin to operate under an open heaven from that day forward Jacob, was blessed with twelve sons.

God promised Jacob, that he would bless him for he was a seed of Abraham. The twelve tribes of Israel come out from his loins that are how Jacob received his name Israel. Remember when Jacob wrestles with the angel (all night).

Genesis 32:24-28 (KJV)

24 And Jacob was left alone; and there wrestled a man with him until the breaking of the day.

25 And when he saw that he prevailed not against him, he touched the hollow of his thigh; and the hollow of Jacob's thigh was out of joint, as he wrestled with him.

26 And he said; let me go, for the day break. And he said; I will not let thee go, until you bless me.

27 And he said unto him, what is thy name? And he said Jacob.

28 And he said, Thy name shall be called no more Jacob, but Israel: for as a prince hast thou power with God and with men, and hast prevailed. Jacob received that name Israel for that name means prince.

Unveiling the Truth about Dreams

First of all we know and have learned that all dreams and visions are not from the Lord we all have dreams which are just nonsense

(Don't make sense), seeing to come from nowhere also need to keep in mind that the enemy will send us dreams as well as visions, he is the great deceiver when we have a dream that seems so real.

How do we know it is from the Lord or not? And visions how we identify with the real from the nonsense dreams. When I first begin to let God cleanse me in my walk with him, he begins to visit me in dreams. I use to always dream of snakes and my car that I had at the time in my life the car would either get stolen, wrecked or returning from out of a place the car would be gone. Sometime I would dream about falling, but I never hit the bottom and I would be awake or wake up from that dream. I believe everyone have dreamed of falling, but never hit the ground. Dreams are a mystery in this mystery we learn that God visit us in dreams and vision when we are asleep everything is quiet and peaceful some of us are dreamers always dreaming.

The First Dream

My first dream was about the Blood of Jesus, me speaking the blood against demonic spirit that had invaded my front yard and they were actually looking like real people. At first as I continue to look at them from my kitchen window they begin to turn into demons marking me. I went to the front door and I didn't know what to do so I ask the Lord what shall I do he said open your mouth I hesitated but as I open my mouth I said the Blood of Jesus! Upon saying those words all of the demons begin to disappear all of them they were sliding in the Power of the Blood of Jesus. It was amazing when I was awaken I felt so good and, refreshed I was so amazed at what had just took place. That was back in 2011 I have not been the same since then I can see the blood of Jesus for what it really is one of our powerful weapons of spiritual warfare. I understand my dreams and God has also given me the gift to interpret dreams.

Acts 2:17-18 (KJV)

17 And it shall come to pass in the last days, saith God; I will pour out of my Spirit upon all flesh: and your sons and your daughters shall prophesy, and your young men shall see visions, and your old men shall dream dreams:

18 And on my servants and on my handmaidens I will pour out in those days of my Spirit; and they shall prophesy:

Second Dream

I was asleep in my bed and I begin to dream I saw myself in the bedroom with people standing around. My brother was there and my kids and some more other relatives. All of a sudden I am pushing and people alone with my brother are helping me to deliver this baby I didn't know I was pregnant. The baby came out it was a boy the baby had on this beautiful blue outfit. After that I got up out of the bed went to the bathroom and washed my face and hands while everyone was admiring this adorable little healthy baby boy.

The Interpretation of the Dream

The bed represent a place of intimacy every room in a house represents something. The people that are standing with me are brothers and sisters in Christ. The kids speak of new beginning, new anointing also, ministry because children come from us they are our ministry. I was pushing in my ministry (boy means strength) in your ministry. The baby having on blue speaks of the Revelation I will have in my ministry and dreams it also is speaking of royalty, colors also have meaning in your dreams. After having the baby I go to the bathroom in a dream the bathroom represent a place of cleansing whether to wash up or to let go waist. It was cleaning me up naturally while God was doing in spiritually (inside). From there I begin to study as much as I could about dreams and interpretation of my dream. I also help others with their interpretation, but all dreams are not from God, but God can still work in anyone life because he is God. Only God can visit you in a dream and tell you what to do or say in the face of evil. Only God can give you a dream about your dreams, gifts, and calling his plans that he has for your life.

Jeremiah 29:11 (KJV)

11 For I know the thoughts that I think toward you, said the Lord, thoughts of peace, and not of evil, to give you an expected end.

Kingdom Training

The Three Sources of Dreams

God dreams which are prophetic soul dreams (emotions) our own dreams Satan comes into our dreams with fears and chasing in dreams. God visit in dreams the dreams of what we call prophetic while asleep he visit in dreams and vision. This is another way God speaks to his people. Dreams are a powerful way to hear from God, with God it is all about the bridegroom vision, dreams, emotions, colors, and numbers they all paint a picture.

Soul Dreams- mind, emotions, and will these are our dreams and desire which comes for our own flesh, angry, lustful thoughts the will wants its own way and desires.

Demonic- evil spirit, darkness, fear, anxiety, snakes, spiders, you get the picture 99% of the dreams are symbolic and 99% of the people in the dreams are symbolic.

God gives warning, instructions, direction through dreams to his bride. Dreams that come from God will always agree with his word. Let's take

Matthew 12:29 (KJV)

29 Or else how can one enter into a strong man's house, and spoil his goods, except he first bind the strong man? And then he will spoil his house.

The house represents aspects about your life the bedroom, living room, kitchen, and bath room. Jesus was always speaking to the people in parables prophetic dreams will always line up with the word of God.

Chapter 4
A Place of Offering

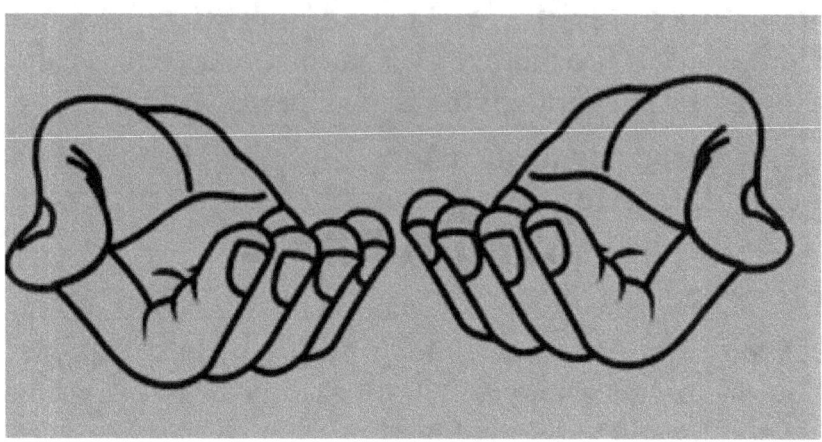

King David purchased a threshing floor to build an altar on it. Why did he buy a threshing floor and not buy a field? Threshing in the Old Testament was harvest time, but this same threshing floor that David purchase was the same threshing floor his great grandmother (Ruth) and Boaz met. The threshing floor was an important place and was often used as landmarks.

A Place of Blessing

Is a place where the grain of harvest was taken from the sower as well as a place where blessing was received?

Numbers 18:30 (KJV)

30 Therefore thou shall say unto them, When ye have heaved the best thereof from it, then it shall be counted unto the Levites as the increase of the threshing floor, and as the increase of the winepress.

Second is picture of a place of judgment.

Matthew 3:12 (KJV)

12 Whose fan is in his hand, he will thoroughly purge his floor, and gather his wheat into the garner; but he will burn up the chaff with unquenchable fire.

On the threshing floor the wheat is separated from the chaff and the tares and the sheaves are beaten or crushed in order to make the separation.

The Temple Site

This is the same location of Mount Moriah were Abraham offer up Isaac.

1st Chronicle 22:1-3(KJV)

1 Then David said, this is the house of the Lord God, and this is the altar of the burnt offering for Israel.

2. So David gave orders to assemble the foreigners residing in Israel, and from among them appointed stonecutters to prepare dressed stone for building the house of God. 3. He provided a large amount of iron to make nails for the doors of the gateways and for the fittings, and more bronze than could be weighed.

Luke 22:31-32 (KJV)

31 And the Lord said, Simon, Simon, behold, Satan hath desired to have you, that he may sift you as wheat:

32 But I have prayed for thee, that thy faith fail not: and when thou art converted, strengthen thy brethren.

God allowed Satan to tempt David and David sinned, revealing his pride and allowing God to deal with him.

Israel Punishment

David had a choice to choose from three punishments

1. Three years of famine
2. Three months of fleeing
3. Or three days of plague

And so David chose one third of the men so the Lord punished Israel with a plague which killed seventy thousand men from Dan in the North of Beer-Sheba in the South. So David saw the angel by the threshing floor his prophet Gad advised him to group and rear an altar unto the Lord, and offered burnt offerings and peace offering. So the Lord was entreated for the land and the plague was stayed from Israel.

 Just as a parent chastises their child so does our heavenly father chastise his children when we are disobedient and rebellious? But he still love us and his mercy endure forever. The threshing floor is a place of prayer.

The Peace Offering

Earlier we touched on the burnt offer, when God instructed Moses, on the offerings that the people and priest were to do in serving in the tabernacle the burnt offer was the first offer.

The peace offering was a thanksgiving offering an offering of sacrifice.

Leviticus 3:1 (KJV)

1 And if his oblation be a sacrifice of peace offering, if of the herd; whether it be a male or female, he shall offer it without blemish before the Lord.

The same blessing that God gave to the prophets of old from Abraham, to John, the Revelator are our promise for today he told Abraham that he would bless his seed and all that are Abraham are blessed with the promises of Abraham.

God has always visit his people in dreams and vision

Deuteronomy 18:18 (KJV)

18 I will raise them up a Prophet from among their brethren, like unto thee, and will put my words in his mouth; and he shall speak unto them all that I shall command him.

Moving On ....

This was just to give a little history and background of where everything begins with Abraham who was a man of faith and obedience. God told Abraham he would be the father of many nations—But God also called Abraham a Prophet there were dreams and angels doing theses times God still speaks through dreams and visions his Word is forever establish in the earth.

Chapter 5

The Prophetic Anointing of a Prophet

Most often when we think about David, we think of the Shepherd boy who became a great king that's the good side. But in taking a closer look at David, we see a man who was a deceiver, a murder, adultery, and a multi law- breaker. (Speaking of the Law of Moses)

Yet the Bible says that David was a man after Gods own heart what a paradox. How can this kind of man be after Gods heart? But the subject of this goes even a step further. Could David, actually be considered one of Gods old testament prophetic? Let's see where the lines converge.

First let's determine what a prophet is. The very first time we find the word prophet used in scriptures is where God speaks to Abimelech in a dream concerning him taking Sarah, to himself. The Lord said, now therefore, restores the man's wife for he is a prophet. As I explained earlier Abraham was a praying prophet (intercessor) and he will pray for you and you will live. But if you do not restore her know that you shall surely die you and all who are grins.

Genesis 20:9 (KJV)

9 Then Abimelech, called Abraham, and said unto him, what hast thou done unto us? And what have I offended thee that thou hast brought on me and on my kingdom a great sin? Thou hast done deeds unto me that ought not to be done.

The Blood Covenant

This was the blood covenant between God and Abraham now remembers David, was of the tribe of Judah. Judah was one of Jacob's sons by his wife Leah.

Genesis 29-35 (KJV)

35 And she conceived again, and bares a son: and she said, Now will I praise the Lord: therefore she called his name Judah; and left bearing.

In the new convent the Lord's life became our life and our life becomes the Lord's life.

Back to David Being a Prophet

The Hebrew term for Prophet is nobly describes someone raised up by God who proclaims what the Lord gave him to say. A true prophet would never contradict the scriptures, nor would he speak from his own mind.

So can David, be counted as a prophet in a true sense of the word, absolutely. David was one of the writing prophets, as we take a look at the book of Psalms written by David, as he talked with the Lord. This is why we should careful search the scriptures all prophets did not go around prophesying. The blessing of David, (the prophet) is our today. There are writes, intercessor just as the prophet of old.

Hear From David a Prophet Heart

Psalm 63:1-2 (NIV)

1 You, God, are my God, earnestly I seek you; I thirst for you, my whole being longs for you, in a dry and parched land where there is no water.

2 I have seen you in the sanctuary and beheld your power and your glory.

It is so ironic how the people whom God choose are the murders, adultery, liars, and cheaters. As I read and such the lives of these people they were not millionaires, they were not perfect people some was so deceiving and manipulating yet God chose them to leave a legacy. This is why we have to be careful how we treat one another we never know if we are entertaining angels. King David was a man after Gods' on heart this is what the bible says about this King as I begin to study the story and life of David I always wondered. Why was it said that he was a man after the heart of God? I found David not only a king, leader, warrior, David was a prophet a man after God heart. Prophets have the heart of God the real prophet, they pick up his burden. Please don't let the word prophet throw you off for they don't always tell you what is going on in your life true prophets are teachers, leaders, and prayer warriors. These are the characteristic of a true Prophet of God this is why David was a man after Gods' own heart.

Chapter 6

A Deeper Walk

As I began to write this one I have so much joy and the tears that comes from this revelation is so unspeakable. We can attend church all our life be raised by Godly people and still miss the mark. As I look back over my own life from a child until now I was raised in what you call Pentecostal/Baptist it became very confusing. The Pentecostal were holy people dancing and shouting the Baptist they did dance or shout they were a more dignified people a little singing, clapping hands and time to pass the plate (collection plate). So growing up in two different worlds was very confusing in my relationship with God.

My Testimony

I grew up a country girl my mom and dad married at a young age back then people married if the female was pregnant at a young age out of fornication they would marry even if they didn't love each other. I lived in two different worlds but I was loved in both you see I was the first born grandchild of both families so they thought I grew up with the love of both sided of my family my mom had plenty of brothers under her and my dad had plenty of brothers under him between them I always had to choose which house I would stay at. I would always pick staying at my daddy, mother's house because they up late but I loved them both sides the same. I had no favorite because they all loved me and I was never a target for mistreatment. Well my mom's mother was saved and filled with the Holy Ghost my daddy mother was not very much of a church going woman both sides of these worlds was so good because there was love from both sides. So I never even thought about who loved God or who didn't I just enjoyed the love and took it in. My granny's always tried to keep the family together when one moved away the other followed. As I grew up I lived more with my parents my dad was a guitar player that was his passion he loved that guitar he could also write music I found this out later on in life. As I started to grow everything begin to change I was beginning to move farther away from the love that was changing but I was changing also.

My First Encounter

My first encounter with the Holy Ghost (spirit) I was about 19 or 20 years old one night my grandmother my dad mother and my aunt went somewhere and I was the driver taking them. On our way back there was this tent meeting we stopped a preacher by the name of Rev. Todd was preaching after his preaching he invited the ones who wanted prayer we went up for prayer he prayed over my grandmother nothing happened.

He prayed for my aunt nothing happen, but when he put his hand on my head and prayed for my something took over my body and I begin to dance, shout, and buck wow! It scared my grandmother and aunt also me but it was my life and I didn't know because no one schooled me on this. Now I went on living my life and completely forgot what happen to me because everyone that I would tell didn't know either. Some said voodoo, some said witchcraft it became of no important to me I went on living my life in the cuter of sin but everything I did even in my wrong doing I was being blessed so I thought.

Pride Will Come

Everything I did good or bad I was always prosper but then I would get proud my pride would say look at my yes see I am truly blessed and you are not as bedded as I am so take that.

Proverbs 16:18 (NIV)

18 Pride goes before destruction and a haughty spirit before a fall.

In a bad sense, pride can mean that someone has an exaggerated sense of good. Someone who is described as proud may be arrogant this was the down fall of Hezekiah.

2nd Chronicle 32:25 (NIV)

25 But Hezekiah's heart was proud and he did not respond to the kindness shown him; therefore the Lord's wrath was on him and on Judah and Jerusalem.

The Worst State

Hitting rock bottom and don't know you have there is a state of deception. So I said in my heart I will not be in the church and be as the hypocrites. They fake, they shake and backbite I rather have been with worldly people thy at least knew what they were doing was wrong still in a state of confusion. For many years I was in this state it is the worst state a person can be in their life.

Proverbs 14:12 (KJV)

12 There is a way which see meth right unto a man, but the end thereof are the ways of death.

James 3:11 (KJV)

11 Doth a fountain send forth at the same place sweet water and bitter?

So many confess that we are all a child of God No! We all were created in the image of God, but to be a true son or daughter one must be born again and sanctify, purified, and set apart for the master use. In other words there must be cleanness in the priesthood in order to walk and operate in the service of a Holy God one have to be clean from all uncleanness of the world, flesh and the devil.

The Life of the Prodigal

After going back to my other world it was a world of drugs, booze, and men's. The worst state, but I was still being blessed so I thought, but the blessing wasn't coming from God. I never knew that the devil could make you prosperous it is a state of deception he comes to steal, kill and destroy. So what was God trying to tell me and I wasn't getting it I thought I knew what I was doing he's not the boss of me this is my life and I do as I please. Wait! Watch out never be critical and judgmental of anyone else because you will find yourself in another zone.

Lost Son

I love this story because a many of us can relate to this. The main character in this parable is the forgiving father.

The younger symbolizes the lost and the older brother represents the self-righteous. It is a picture of restoration of a believer into fellowship with or back to the father.

What I was lacking in my life with the father was a relationship Jesus is the way, the truth and the life and no one can come to the father, bur through him.

A relationship with him is very important as a father to a son. This is a relationship I desired with my natural dad, but never had that closeness so I had no clue my heavenly father desire to have a relationship with me my family had become dysfunctional, but God, was always there.

After coming back to him I was so tired of in and out I begin to seek him for myself. I want you to know that God, desire to have a personal one on one relationship with you there are things that he wants to tell you and show you that no one else can do. Come back to the fold.

Fellowship with God

1st John 1:3 (KJV)

3 That which we have seen and heard declares unto you, that ye also may have fellowship with us: and truly our fellowship is with the Father and with his a Son Jesus Christ.

Fellowship with God was one of the richest privileges before the fall man. The Lord God walked in the garden and talked with Adam, as a man talk with his friend. Long as he was willing and obedient Adam ate the fat of the land he had an unbroken communion with God, his father. Sin separate us from fellowship (communicate) with God. We are moved so far away from him and live in a state of deception that we are in good standing with the father in the presence of a Holy God there can't be sin he is Holy that is one of his characters.

On Judah and Jerusalem

It is one thing to be in your pride zone in the world, but when in your pride zone in church (Christ) it is a death sentence. After years passed married into a family God still dealing with me I still didn't listen to what God was trying to tell me in. Still in my mess doing the same old things but in the service of the Lord, yes I knew something wasn't right, but I had no clued what? I knew my life was a seesaw up and down for so many years, but get this I was still confused even in Christ. So I tried to live right on my own it didn't work I got frustrated and returned back into the world just as they expected me to just as I thought. Now the enemy comes seven times bringing seven more spirits worse than the first state you were in.

Matthew 12:43-45 (ASV)

43 But the unclean spirit, when he is gone out of the man, passed through waterless places, seeking rest, and find it not.

44 Then he said, I will return into my house whence I came out; and when he is come, he find it empty, swept, and garnished.

45 Then go him, and take with himself seven other spirits more evil than himself, and they enter in and dwell there: and the last state of that man becomes worse than the first. Even so shall it be also unto this evil generation.

Chapter 7

David Charge to Solomon

Then he called for Salomon his son, and charged him to build an house for the Lord God of Israel and David said to Solomon, my son, as for me, it was in my mind to build an house unto the name of the Lord my God: But the word of the Lord came to me saying, thou hast shed blood abundantly, and has made great wars; thou shall not build an house unto my name, because thou hast shed much blood upon the earth in my sight.

Behold, a son shall be born to thee, who shall be a man of rest; and I will give him rest from all his enemies round about: for his name shall be Solomon and I will give peace and quietness unto Israel in his days.

He shall build a house for my name; and he shall be my son, and I will be his father, and I will establish the throne of his kingdom over Israel forever.

Building of the Temple

2nd Chronicles 3:1 (KJV)

1Then Solomon, began to build the house of the Lord at Jerusalem in Mount Moriah where the Lord appeared unto David, his father in the place that David, had prepared in the threshing floor of the Jebusite.

King Solomon had the same gifting and talents as his father King David. He was a writer, a king and I think it's safe to say he was a prophet and priest.

2nd Chronicles 2:6-7 (KJV)

6 And Solomon went up thither to the brazen altar before the Lord, which was at the tabernacle of the congregation, and offered a thousand burnt offerings upon it.

7 In that night did God appear unto Solomon, and said unto him, Ask what I shall give thee

Solomon talked with the father and he made his request known. Now David, being the son of Jesse and the great grandson of Ruth, Solomon is the great, great grandson of Ruth.

Let's remember in the book of Genesis 22:2 say that God told Abraham to take his son Isaac into the land of Mariah and to offer him there for a burnt offering.

Here we see this is the same place that Solomon, is building the first temple in the same place where it first began.

We have traced the beginning of the threshing floor from Abraham to Solomon lets continue to move forward with our Prophetic inheritance from the beginning until the end.

The Wisdom of the King

2nd Chronicles 1:10-12

10 Give me now wisdom and knowledge that I may go out and come in before this people: for who can judge this thy people that is so great?

11 And God said to Solomon, Because this was in thine heart, and thou hast not asked riches, wealth, or honor, nor the life of thy enemies, neither yet hast asked long life; but hast asked wisdom and knowledge for thyself, that thou may judge my people, over whom I have made thee king:

12 Wisdom and knowledge is granted unto thee; I will give thee riches, and wealth, and honor, such as none of the kings have had that have been before thee, neither shall there any after thee have the like.

Under the New Covenant

We are kings and priest to operate in the wisdom and knowledge of God in his kingdom. We are destiny to rule and reign upon the earth.

We can learn when we seek God with all our heart he will be found, those who honor God will be honored. God will equip us to accomplish the task he calls us to if we will rely on him. The day will come, says the Lord, when I will make a new covenant with the people of Israel and Judah...

Jeremiah 31:33 (NKJV)

33 But this is the covenant that I will make with the house of Israel after those days, I will put my law in their minds, and write it on their hearts; and I will be their God, and they shall be my people.

The old covenant was written in our hearts only through

Jesus Christ who shed his blood for the sins of the world.

We are on our way to the cross we cannot share the inheritance of Jesus Christ

Roman 8:17 (KJV)

17 And if children, then heirs; heirs of God, and joint-heirs with Christ; if so be that we suffer with him, that we may be also glorified together.

The Holy Place

1st Peter 2:9 (KJV)

9 But you are a chosen generation, a royal priesthood, a holy nation, a peculiar people; that ye should show forth the praises of him who hath called you out of darkness into the marvelous light.

The altar was three feet in height alone with the Ark of the Covenant. The altar of incense is where the priest worshiped (ministered) to God commune with him this was Gods pattern. This is where prayer, intersession and worship were done in the office of the priest.

Exodus 30:1-3; 7-8 (NIV)

1 Make an altar of acacia wood for burning incense.

2 It is to be a square, a cubit long and a cubit wide, and two cubits high- its horns of one piece with it.

3 Overlay the top and all the sides and the horns with pure gold, and make gold, and make a gold molding around it.

7 Aaron must burn fragrant incense on the altar every morning when he tends the lamps.

8 He must burn incense again when he lights the lamps at

twilight so incense will burn regularly before the Lord for the generations to come.

In the holy place was the Monarch, shewbread altar of incense.

Jesus Cleanse the Temple

I use to always wonder why Jesus was so angry when he came to the temple and overturned the tables and said my father house should be a house of prayer, after tracing the importance of this temple from Abraham, day to Jesus day I begin to understand a very sacred place.

When we look back at the prophet Jeremiah, his reaction was the same Jeremiah, was always going to the temple proclaiming the word of God to the priest who were out of order in the service of the Lord. God had a pattern he gave to Moses, in the wilderness to follow his pattern is still for us today, but we don't have to go the temple we are the temple of the living God.

Chapter 8

Over Shadow Me

Luke 1:35-36 (KJV)

35 And the angel answered and said unto her, The Holy Ghost shall come upon thee, and the power of the Highest shall overshadow thee: therefore also that holy thing which shall be born of thee shall be called the Son of God.

36 And behold thy cousin Elizabeth, she has also conceived a son in her old age and this is the six month with her who was called barren.

Luke 1:5-9 (KJV)

5 There was in the day of Herod; the king of Judaea, a certain priest named Zacharias, of the course of Abia: and his wife was of the daughters of Aaron, and her name was Elisabeth.

6 And they were both righteous before God, walking in all the commandments and ordinances of the Lord blameless.

7 And they had no child, because that Elisabeth was barren, and they both were now well stricken in years

8 And it came to pass, that while he executed the priest's office before God in the order of his course,

9 According to the custom of the priest's office, his lot was to burn incense when he went into the temple of the Lord.

The Altar of Incense

God gave Moses, the instructions to make an altar of incense in the Old Testament so the priest could come in the Holy Place. In the Holy Place where the shewbread, and the monarch.

Jesus Called the Lamb of God

When Mary, was overshadow by the Holy Ghost she was a virgin pure never knew a man. Jesus is called the Lamb of God without any contamination, pure; his blood was free from any human bodily fluids. This is why he is called the Lamb of God his blood washed away all impurities (sin). Ask the Holy Spirit to overshadow you so when he come upon you and overshadow you, you will become impregnated with the dreams, vision and fruits of the spirit which is the promise of the Father. Mary was overshadowed with promise we also have a spiritual inheritance that will overshadow us if we let it.

Jesus was the ultimate sacrifice for sin in the Old Testament the sacrifice for sin played a very important role in the Jewish religion. The priest would slay a Lamb take the blood and spread it on the altar the Bronze Altar. It is through his death on the cross he is God's perfect sacrifice for sin and his resurrection on the cross. God has provided the offering that atones for our sin this is the good news of the Gospel. God raised him from the dead he is the Lamb of God who take away the sins of the world.

John 3:16

16 For God so loved the world that he gave his only begotten Son, that whosoever believeth in him should not perish, but have everlasting life.

No more animal's sheep's, goats, heifers, and rams no more going through man for atonements for our sins Jesus is the precious Lamb of God It is finish the finish work of the cross.

Warfare in the Heavenly

Revelation 12:7-10

7 And there was war in heaven: Michael and his angels fought against the dragon; and the dragon fought and his angels,

8 And prevailed not; neither was their place found any more in heaven.

9 And the great dragon was cast out, that old serpent, called the Devil, and Satan, which deceived the whole world: he was cast out into the earth, and his angels were cast out with him.

10 And I heard a loud voice saying in heaven, now cometh salvation, and strength, and the kingdom of our God, and the power of his Christ: for the accuser of our brethren is cast down, which accused them before our God day and night.

As Lucifer was God's main worshipper he was full of beauty and had all of the instruments within him. He was lifted up with pride and decided he wanted to be not just like God, but he wanted to be God. He wanted to be the God of the universe and had plans of taking God's throne. He persuaded about one-third of all the other angels to go to war against God.

What was he thinking? Taking matters into his own hands. We are talking about the all mighty, all powerful all knowing God of creation.

"O Lucifer son of the morning" how ant thou fallen from heaven we were created to worship him.

Ezekiel 28:17 (AMP)

17 Your heart was proud and up because of your beauty, you corrupted your wisdom for sake of splendor. I cast you to the ground; I lay you before kings that they might eat.

Isaiah 14: 13-14 (KJV)

13 And you said in your heart, I will ascend to heaven; I will exalt my throne above the stars of God; I will sit upon the mount of assembly in the uttermost north.

14 I will ascend above the heights of the clouds; I will make myself like the Most High.

Making know to us the mystery (secret) of his will (of his plan, of his purpose). God's ultimate well is to have all things subjected to Jesus. His grandmaster plan is for Jesus to rule over everything both in heaven and earth. We have a helper on earth which is the Holy Spirit now that the Holy Spirit is here on the earth, Jesus must remain in the heaven until Satan and his army is thrown out of heaven. In order for Jesus to rule over everything he is going to have to defeat his enemies that are the spiritual forces of wickedness that are positioned in heaven.

Chapter 9

Understanding the Prophetic

A. Prophecy

The testimony of Jesus Christ is the spirit of Prophecy

The gift of prophecy

Revelation 19:10 (KJV)

10 And I fell at his feet to worship him. And he said unto me, See thou do it not: I am thy fellow servant, and of thy brethren that have the testimony of Jesus: worship God: for the testimony of Jesus is the spirit of prophecy.

The gifts of the Holy Spirit offer to us as believer the gift of prophecy. God is building a prophetic church with kingdom mindset. The gift of the spirit need to be operating in the body of Christ to bring his church to maturity alone with the gift of prophecy the fruit of the spirit needs to also be operating in our lives. The prophets of old as well as the New Testament prophet, prophesized about the things of God concerning his son and the Israelites

The revelation of Jesus Christ which God gave him to show to his servant the things that must soon take place. He made it known by sending his angel to his servant John who bore witness to the word of God and to the testimony of Jesus Christ, even to all that he saw. Blessed is the one who needs aloud the word of this prophecy, and blessed are those who hear, and who keep what is written in it for the time is near.

B. Prophetic Ministry

The Five Fold Ministry- This is the ministry Jesus gives

The prophetic ministry is tied in with the fivefold.

Ephesians 4:11 (KJV)

11 And he gave some, apostles; and some prophets; and evangelists; and some pastors and teachers.

This is God's order for his divine government in the body of Christ unfortunately his body is not operating under this order it has become a one man show and we aren't growing in the kingdom of God. Let's look farther what he says;

Ephesians 4:12-14 (KJV)

12 For the perfecting of the saints, for the work of the ministry, for the edifying of the body of Christ:

13 Till all come in the unity of the faith, and of the knowledge of the Son of God, unto a perfect man, unto the measure of the stature of the fullness of Christ:

14 That we henceforth be no more children, tossed to and fro, and carried about with every wind of doctrine, by the sleight of men, and cunning craftiness, whereby they lie in wait to deceive.

Wow! Some of us need to let go and let God! This prophetic ministry was given by Jesus and under the tutor of Jesus Christ.

C. Office of the Prophet

The office of the prophet is under the direction of God the Father. This is a government position in the body of Christ; God will confirm that calling to this office.

Romans 12: 6-8 (KJV)

6 Having then gifts differing according to the grace that is given to us, whether prophecy, let us prophesy according to the proportion of faith;

7 Or ministry let us wait on our ministering: or he that teaches, on teaching;

8 Or he that exhorted, on exhortation: he gives, let him do it with simplicity; he that rules, with diligence; he that show mercy, with cheerfulness.

You will be totally consumed by God and die to all that you are or ever will be because you love the Lord and all his servants totally being consumed by God. He will purify you, sanctify you to holiness. He will refine you in the refiner so you will be refined as pure gold with no impurities no this process is not easy it is a beating and purging. Many times you will say ouch! Know whatever the Lord gives you, you will have to walk it out.

Chapter 10

Standing In the Gap: Intercessory Prayer

Ezekiel 22:30 (NIV)

30 I looked for someone among them who would build up the wall and stand before me in the gap on behalf of the land so I would not have to destroy it, but I found no one.

This kind of prayer requires commitment on the part of the person praying.

It is a request that is brought before the Lord maybe many times until the person that is prayed for get or see results.

The word intercede comes from the Latin word (inter) meaning between and cede meaning (go between) intercede (stand between).

So the one who is praying is standing between the person being prayed for on their behalf reaching to God for the person need to be met or answered the need could be physically, spiritual, emotional, or financial.

Whatever the need is the one standing in the gap for the answer from God should pray until the pray is answered maybe day 1, maybe day 2, maybe more it is a commitment on the intercessor part.

Revelation: The Court Room (Part 1)

As I was praying for someone God gave me a revelation that blew me away a vision. In your interceding on behalf of another you are in a court room where God is the judge and you are the defending attorney. I knew nothing about law in this sense we presented the person case to God pleading for an answer coming in the name of Jesus.

But there is an opposing one which is the enemy (Satan) but God has giving us all of the powerful weapon we need to present our case unto him that the one who we are standing in the gap for can get an answer and be set free this awesome!

Isaiah 59:16 (KJV)

16 And he saw that there was no man, and wondered that there was no intercessor: therefore his arm brought salvation unto him; and his righteousness, it sustained him.

Standing in the gap is not a popular job because one is called to lay down their life in prayer for others.

The spirit of intercession is praying for mercy and forgiveness for others.

Standing in the gap interceding is a powerful weapon.

Revelation: The Court Room (Part 2)

God is the judge the intercessor comes before God (judge) on behalf of the person praying about it. It's like the prayer warrior is the lawyer the prayer warrior present his/her case (request) to God on behalf of the person being prayed for there is another in the court room who is opposing of this request for the person being prayed for but with the weapons that God gives to use in your prayer request (case) for the one you are standing in the gap for God approves your request and the person prayer is answered all because you stood in the gap and pleaded his/her case. Because this is spiritual it happens in the spiritual realm before it manifest in the natural.

Praise Is What I Do

The Purpose of Our Praise and Worship

The purpose of our praise and worship is to glorify, honor, praise, exalt, and please God. Our worship must show an adoration and loyalty to God for his grace in providing us with the way to escape the bondage of sin so we can have the salvation he so much wants to give us.

Establish who God is:

1. Justice - God will make everything alright when you are mistreated because of his justice nature.

2. Goodness – God is good, he is good all the time even when we do wrong and don't deserve it.

3. Holiness – God is Holy, what does that mean (righteous) his majesty always right and perfect moral, purity, clean <Absolutely No Sign> or evil thought.

4. Sovereign – He rules, means he does what he wants no one tell him how and when to do. He can't be bought or manipulated the all-powerful God is in control of everything of what even happen good or bad.

5. Trinity – He is the Father, Son, and the Holy Ghost he reveals himself in three person though he is one.

6. Omniscience – God possess perfect knowledge and

therefore has no need to learn, (all knowing) God knows everything it is impossible to hide anything from him-he knows our every thought.

The atmosphere has to be set in order to work God is in or you? You are ushered into his presence he is seeker for those that will give him this place in their life an awesome worshippers praise and worship is the heart of the church.

Acts 16:25-34 (KJV)

25 And at midnight Paul and Silas prayed, and sang praises unto God: and the prisoners heard them.

26 And suddenly there was a great earthquake, so that the foundations of the prison were shaken: and immediately (all) the doors were opened, and every one's bands were loosed.

27 And the keeper of the prison awaking out of his sleep, and seeing the prison doors open, he drew out his sword, and would have killed himself, supposing that the prisoners had been fled.

28 But Paul cried with a loud voice, saying, Do thyself no harm: for we are all here.

29 Then he called for a light, and fell down before Paul and Silas,

30 And brought them out, and said, Sirs, what must I do to be saved?

31 And they said, Believe on the Lord Jesus Christ, and thou shall be saved, and thy house.

32 And they spoke unto him the word of the Lord, and to all that were in his house.

33 And he took them the same hour of the night, and washed their stripes; and was baptized, he and all his straightway.

34 And when he had brought them into his house, he set meat before them, and rejoiced, believing in God with his entire house.

All we have to do is get back to the basic of the church and obey God and his word then we will see a might move of God.

Earthquake – A sudden and violent shaking of the ground, sometimes causing great destruction as a result of movement within the earth's crust or volcano action

(Spiritual Earthquakes) shake, rattle and roll you.

The Lion of the Tribe of Judah

Revelation 5:5 (KJV)

5 And one of the elders said unto me, Weep not: behold, the Lion of the tribe of Judah, the Root of David, hath prevailed to open the book, and to lose the seven seals thereof.

Genesis 29:35 (KJV)

(Judah means praise)

35 And she conceived again, and bares a son: and she said, Now will I praise the Lord: therefore she called his name Judah; and left bearing.

Psalms 150:1-6 (KJV)

1 Praise ye the Lord. Praise God in his sanctuary: praise him in the firmament of his power.

2 Praise him for his mighty acts: praise him according to his excellent greatness.

3 Praise him with the sound of the trumpet: praise him with the psaltery and harp.

4 Praise him with the tumbrel and dance: praise him with stringed instruments and organs.

5 Praise him upon the loud cymbals: praise him upon the high sounding cymbals.

6 Let everything that hath breath praise the Lord. Praise ye the Lord.

James 4:6; 10 (KJV)

6 But he gives more grace. Wherefore he said, God resisted the proud, but gives grace unto the humble.

10 Humble yourselves in the sight of the Lord, and he shall lift you up.

John 4:23-24 (KJV)

23 But the hour cometh and now is, when the true worshippers shall worship the Father in spirit and in truth: for the Father seek such to worship him.

24 God is a (Spirit) and they that worship him must worship him (in spirit) and (in truth).

(Must) is not an optional God seeks true worshippers

Jeremiah 10:23 (KJV)

23 O Lord, I know that the way if man is not in himself: it is not in man that walked to direct his steps.

Worship is a time when we pay deep sincere, awesome respect, love, and fear to the one who created us.

Acts 17:24-25 (KJV)

24 God that made the world and all things therein, seeing that he is Lord of heaven and earth, dwell not in temples made with hands;

25 Neither is worshipped with men's hands, as though he needed anything, seeing he gives to all life, and breath, and all things; God is the one who holds our eternal destiny in his hand.

Philippians 2:12

12 Wherefore, my beloved, as ye have always obeyed, not as in my presence only, but now much more in my absence, work out your own salvation with fear and trembling.

"Draw near to God and he will draw near to you!"

Worship helps us develop a God-like and Christ-like character

Our worship not only honors and magnifies God but it is also for our own edification and strength.

Worship helps to develop God and Christ like character.

Philippians 2:5 (KJV)

5 Let this mind be in you, which was also in Christ Jesus:

Romans 12:2 (KJV)

2 And be not conformed to this world: but be transformed by the renewing of your mind that you may prove what that good acceptable and perfect will of God is.

God resist the proud

Colossians 3:2 (KJV)

2 Set your affection on things above, not on things on the earth.

Chapter 11

Power of The Cross

The gospel writers reported that Jesus was crucified at a place of a skull, known as Golgotha in Hebrew meaning skull near the old city of Jerusalem cavities a rocky hillside align to form a vivid image of a skull.

Matthew 27:47-53 (KJV)

47 Some of them that stood there, when they heard that, said this man call for Elias.

48 And straightway one of them ran, and took a sponge, and filled it with vinegar, and put it on a reed, and gave him to drink.

49 The rest said, Let be, let us see whether Elias will come to save him.

50 Jesus, when he had cried again with a loud voice, yielded up the ghost.

51 And behold, the veil of the temple was rent in twain (two) from top to bottom; and the earth did quake, and the rocks rent.

52 And the graves were opened; and many bodies of the saints which slept arose,

53 And came out of the graves after his resurrection, and went into the holy city, and appeared unto many.

We must embrace the power of the cross he came to save all that which was lost from the natural to our spiritual inheritance. As we seen in Chapter 1 where Abraham was on Mt. Mariah with Isaac it was a picture of Jesus Christ being the sacrifice for the sins of the world.

It takes the cross to redeem mankind, in our study of this subject where Abraham offers his only son at Moriah. We talked about Ruth and Boaz; we went to where it all begins with Abraham and Isaac.

From there we picked up Jacob, Abraham's grandson we study Lot's daughters in their trickery.

Then we study King David, who purchased the threshing floor and Solomon, Who built the temple on the threshing floor his father David purchased.

From there we got to Zechariah the priest with Mary and Elizabeth.

Now we come to our Lord and Savior Jesus Christ as he goes to the temple and cleanse the temple the same temple that Solomon built, but we know that the temple had to be rebuilt in the Prophet Zechariah days the rebuilding of the temple we establish that everyone that had a part in this study were prophets and it is prophetic because everything was orchestrate by God.

It's Prophetic

Bible scholar's states that Jesus was on the cross outside of Jerusalem not far from the temple a place call the skull on a mountain or hill.

Jesus came to restore, redeem mankind back to his originally state before the fall of Adam and Eve.

The power of the cross he defeated Satan with his blood, he beat death with his blood, he restored man back to the father with his blood,

Hebrews 9:22 (KJV)

22 He redeemed man with his blood, without the shedding of blood there is no forgiveness of sin.

There is power in the pure unadulterated blood of Jesus and it has become our inheritance in Christ Jesus.

Embrace the cross no greater love than for a man to lay down his life for a friend.

His name is Jesus what a might awesome God we serve.

HE has risen from the dead, and it is finished.

Dream about the Blood

I had a dream while I was asleep God visited me to show me how to do warfare by the blood. I saw myself with my family in the kitchen of the house I was living at that time.

I was looking out the window and I saw a gang of men walking by and around my fence. As I looked they begin to look back at me while I was in the window all of a sudden the more I looked at them they begin to change into demons I looked and they began to mock me.

One of my daughters asked me what or you going to do mama. I stormed from the kitchen to the living room and she tried to stop me but I insisted I was going to the door.

I had no idea what I was going to do or say all I knew was they were in my yard and I wanted them out.

I open the door and stood there gazing I said to myself what do I do Lord he said open your mouth. I hesitated at first but I open up my mouth and I said "The Blood of Jesus" when I said the Blood of Jesus those demons begin to slide and disappear one by one.

You see I had no idea that there was such power in the blood, but we can do warfare with the blood, no one even taught that, some never gave that much attention to give this truth about the powerful blood of Jesus.

Some don't mention the power of the blood until Easter Sunday, but there will be an account given on judgment day for what is known and not taught. This is another reason we should embrace the cross his blood

Hebrews 10:19-22 (KJV)

19 Having therefore, brethren, boldness to enter into the holiest by the blood of Jesus,

20 By a new and living way, which he hath consecrated for us, through the veil, that is to say, his flesh;

21 And having a high priest over the house of God;

22 Let us draw near with a true heart in full assurance of faith, having our hearts sprinkled from an evil conscience, and our bodies washed with pure water.

Sanctification through the Blood

The new life through the blood Christ gave himself for the church that he might sanctify it, having cleansed it.

Ephesians 4:25 (KJV)

25 Wherefore putting away lying, speaks every man truth with his neighbor: for we are members one of another.

It was because of his death that we are sanctified; through his suffering in the cross (blood) sanctification is deep people.

You are mankind by his blood, The Blood of Jesus, The Blood Speaks with Divine life giving power.

"May the very God of peace sanctify you wholly?"

Amen.

To Serve the Living God

So we have this fellowship to come into with God through the blood.

Ephesians 2:13 (KJV)

13 But now in Christ Jesus ye who sometimes were far off are made nigh by the blood of Christ.

Hebrews 9:14 (KJV)

14 How much more shall the blood of Christ, who through the eternal Spirit offered himself without spot to God, purge your conscience from dead works to serve the living God?

Chapter 12

The Mantle

Mantle – A loose sleeveless cloak or shawl, worn especially by women.

Jeremiah 33:3 (KJV)

3 Call unto me, and I will answer thee, and show the great and mighty things, which thou knows not.

Wailing Woman

This is a battle cry Jeremiah said to call for the mourning women. When the Lord calls for women the situation is getting out of hands and need emergent intervention he was called a weeping prophet, but the present situation was beyond male teens God need a woman's tears.

The term cunning means (skillfulness) the ability to produce something.

The church (body of Christ) has the ability to produce the life of Christ, but we are at ease.

As I stated before this is a battle cry he is calling for the wailing women to morn, weep wail in the face of the adversity.

It is time for the body to answer the call to wail.

A prophetic tear over the nation speaks powerful in the site of a Sovereign God.

Take Up Your Mantle

After the renewal by the Lord on Mount Horeb, Elijah began a ministry of mentoring or disciplines Elisha.

Mentoring or discipline others is one of the most important ministries any of us can especially leaders, but one that should not be limited to leaders.

1 King 19:19-21 (KJV)

19 So he departed thence, and found Elisha the son of Shaphat, who was plowing with twelve yoke of oxen before him, and he with the twelfth: and Elijah passed by him, and cast his mantle upon him.

20 And he left the oxen, and ran after Elijah, and said, let me, I pray thee, kiss my father and my mother, and then I will follow thee. And he said unto him, Go back again: for what have I done to thee?

21 And he returned back from him, and took a yoke of oxen, and slew them, and boiled their flesh with the instruments of the oxen, and gave unto the people, and they did eat. Then he arose, and went after Elijah, and ministered unto him.

Man-date

The word means a commission to do something assign (territory) under a mandate of the League of Nations.

The mandate comes from the Holy Spirit after the mantle then comes the mandate the (assignment) because the

Lord has to equip you to go into the world, to other nations to preach the gospel of Jesus Christ.

Go into the world and preach the Gospel (the good news) to every creature. He that believe and is baptize shall be saved; but he that believeth not shall be dammed.

Mark 16:15-16 (KJV)

15 And he said unto them, Go ye into the entire world, and preach the gospel (the good news) to every creature.

16 He that believeth and is baptized shall be saved; but he that believeth not shall be damned. "Jesus; said it is finish!"

Take up your mandate and go preach, teach make true disciples of all men only what we do for Christ will last.

In my writing on the Prophetic I want to point out to you that every prophet that God called to service God either spoken directly to them or he visited them in dreams. So many take the simple gift of prophecy that the Holy Spirit is signifying to us that this is where the confusion comes into the body of Christ one can have the gift of prophecy, and not be called to the ministry or office of a prophet.

Let us start with the Major Prophets my goal is to prove and show that every prophet had either a dream, vision or the word or all three operating in their life.

E-li-jah- As I study the life of Elijah, there was no evidence that God appeared to him in dreams or vision but the scriptures always state the word of the Lord. The Lord, came to Elijah, this prophet had direct contact with God because of his dynamic prayer life.

Elijah prayed for rain to stop, rain to start he even called fire down from heaven.

1 King 17:1

1 And Elijah the Tishbite, who was of the inhabitants of Gilead, said unto Ahab, As the Lord God of Israel liveth, before whom I stand; there shall not be dew nor rain these years, but according to my word.

But what we do know about Elijah he had a school of the prophets.

1 Samuel 10:11; 19:19 (KJV)

11 And it came to pass, when all that knew him beforetime saw that, behold, he prophesied among the prophets, then the people said one to another, What is this that is come unto the son of Kish? Is Saul also among the prophets?

19 And it was told Saul, saying, Behold, David is at Naioth in Ramah.

1 Samuel 10:6, 10 (KJV)

6 And the Spirit of the Lord will come upon thee, and thou shall prophesy with them, and shall be turned into another man.

10 And when they came thither to the hill, behold a company of prophets met him; and the Spirit of God came upon him, and he prophesied among them.

King Saul prophesized when the Spirit of the Lord came upon him. Saul was called to be a king not a prophet, but the Spirit does as it will.

The Prophet Samuel

Samuel did not have dreams or vision, but the word of the Lord came to him as he ministered unto the Lord.

And the child Samuel ministered unto the Lord before E' li. And the word of the Lord was precious in those days, there were no open visions.

The prophet and teachers at Antioch were ministering unto the Lord through their praise and worship.

Ministering to the Lord why would he speak to us in our personal time with him in fellowship.

The Prophet Isaiah

Let's take a look at this prophet life how God appeared and spoke to him.

Isaiah 1:1 (KJV)

1 The vision of Isaiah the son of Amos, which he saw concerning Judah and Jerusalem in the days of Uzziah, Jotham, Ahaz, and Hezekiah, kings of Judah.

Notice that the vision Isaiah, saw was concerning the things of God not of man (human). Judah was in heavy idolatry the prophet called to service to turn the hearts of God's people back to God.

The Prophet Jeremiah

Jeremiah 1:4; 14:14 (KJV)

4 Then the word of the Lord came unto me, saying.

14 Then the Lord said unto me, the prophets prophesy lies in my name: I sent them not, neither have I commanded them, neither spoke unto them, they prophesy unto you a false vision and divination, and a thing of naught, and the deceit of their heart.

And we will give two more prophets Ezekiel and Daniel.

Ezekiel 1:1-3 (KJV)

1 Now it came to pass in the thirtieth year, in the fourth month, in the fifth day of the month, I was among the captives by the river of Chebar, that the heavens were opened, and I saw visions of God.

And he goes on to say in verse 3,

3 The word of the Lord came expressly unto Ezekiel the priest, the son of Buzi, in the land of Chaldeans by the river Chebar; and the hand of the Lord was there upon him.

Ezekiel was first a priest and became a prophet so he was both priest and prophet.

Daniel, this prophet was also a praying prophet but let's take a look to see what the word says about Daniel.

Daniel 7:1 (KJV)

1 In the first year of Belshazzar king of Babylon Daniel had a dream and visions of his head upon his bed: then he wrote the dream, and told the sum of the matters.

John- (Revelation) Nearly the entire book of Revelation is a vision John, had while exiled on the island of Patmos. John's vision explains in more details some of the events that God had shown Daniel.

Today's dreams and visions with the completion of the bible they are complete there are no new Revelation of visions and dreams. The prophecy has been sealed (closed) now we have the word of God to search the scriptures for our decision and answers to what we need. God can communicate how he chooses he is God. Now our dreams and visions are more personal toward us he visits us while we are asleep.

This is just an overview of the truth of God's word and how he communicates with his people through his dreams, visions and his word, but we are to rely on his word for everything we do if the dreams and visions don't line up with the word of God then we ourselves do injustice.

I just want to take this time to invite you to accept Jesus today as your personal Lord and Savior. He is standing at the door of your heart knocking and wanting to come in just say this prayer with me.

Dear God of heaven, I come to you in the name of Jesus. I acknowledge that I am a sinner I am sorry for my sins and the life I have lived I need your forgiveness. I believe that you sent Jesus your only begotten son to die and shed his precious blood on the cross at Calvary for my sins. I am willing and ready to turn from sins.

You said in your Holy word that if I confess to the Lord and believe in my heart the God raised Jesus from the dead, I shall be saved.

Now I confess Jesus as my Savior and believe in my heart you raised him from the dead I thank you for hearing my pray to forgive and save me.

Not only do I want to be saved I also want to be born again by your Holy Spirit so my life can be change so I can have fellowship with you through your Holy Spirit.

John 3:5 (KJV)

5 Jesus answered, Verily, verily; I say unto thee, except a man is born of water and of the Spirit, he cannot enter into the kingdom of God.

Understanding How to Operate in the Prophetic:

Are you struggling with understanding the prophetic and prophesies in the bible?

Are you struggling with your gifts and calling, and identity in Christ?

Are you ready to know who you are in him and your purpose in the kingdom of God?

Operating Under the Prophetic

(1) Walking in the prophetic which comes from the third realm of the heavens, which is the kingdom of God.

(2) God wants you to know who you are in Christ Jesus your true identity in him.

(3) Appling the basic biblical principle to your life follow the patriarchs in the Old Testament who walked in the prophetic (obedience) of God.

Here Comes the Bride

Discover the Truth about the True Church of the Living God......

The Mystery which is the things of God that he is revealing to his people in these last and evil days.

The early church did not have the problems that we have today with the many different concepts taught in the body of Christ. The first church (century) apostles was taught by Christ himself and believed the same thing they set the foundation on for the church, the doctrine of the Gospel of Jesus Christ- we the body are to take up were they left off the foundation has already been laid.

Ephesians 2:19-20 (KJV)

19 Now therefore ye are no more strangers and foreigners, but fellow citizens with the saints, and of the household of God;

20 And are built upon the foundation of the apostles and prophets, Jesus Christ himself being the chief corner stone.

The Fivefold Ministry

Ephesians 4:11-13 (ASV)

11 And he gave some to be apostles; and some, prophets; and some, evangelists; and some, pastors and teachers;

12 For the perfecting of the saints, unto the work of ministering unto the building up or the body of Christ:

13 Till we all attain unto the unity of faith, and of the knowledge of the Son of God, unto a full-grown man, unto the measure of the stature of the fullness of Christ.

Order of Service

Prayer was always the main order of service in the early church. They all joined together constantly in prayer. They recognized the great truth that the Christian church is one big happy family; and each one supplied and fulfilled their duties as a member of the whole body in order to provide what was needed and contribute to the edification of the body, the edification of the church and prayed on one accord.

Acts 14:1 (KJV)

1These all continued with one accord in prayer and supplication with the women, and Mary the mother of Jesus, and with his brethren.

Acts 2:46-47 (KJV)

46 And they, continuing daily with one accord in the temple, and breaking bread from house to house, did eat their meat with gladness and singleness of heart,

47. Praising God and having favor with all the people. And the Lord added to the church daily such as should be saved.

Supplication (as known as petitioning) is a form of prayer, wherein one party humbly or earnestly asks another party to provide something; either for the party who is doing the supplicating (e.g. "Please spare my life." Or on behalf of someone else (e.g. "Please spare my child's life.").

So a prayer of supplication is asking God for something, unlike the prayer of petition is praying on behalf of others the prayer of supplication is generally a request for the person prayer they knew how to pray.

The Words of Our Testimony

Revelation 12:11 (KJV)

11 And they overcame him by the blood of the Lamb and by the word of their testimony; and they loved not their lives unto the death.

The early church gave the testimony of the goodness of God, his mercy his forgiveness of sin and how Jesus had delivered them from their sins they were a witness that Jesus Christ had come into the world in human flesh. When God begin to deal with me about the foundation and order of the church he said my people do not testify about my forgiveness of sin anymore they only give praise report and call it a testimony or they give a praise report of another and call it a testimony.

When Jesus saved and delivered me from my sins my

testimony was how he delivered me from drugs, alcohol, cigarettes a mighty testimony of what the Lord Jesus the son of God the Lamb of God did in my life.

On the road to Damascus Saul, had an encounter with Jesus, suddenly a bright light shone on Saul, causing his entire party to fall to the ground. Then Jesus spoke to Saul, asking him "why are you persecuting me?" Having a personal encounter with Jesus Christ gave the believer a testimony of the Lord and Savior Jesus Christ.

Testimonies have been taken out of some of the churches this is how the early church function let us not lose our testimony of how we first had our glorious encounter with Jesus Christ. He transferred you out of darkness and placed you into his marvelous light he has done great things since this is where the glorious journey began. Let us hold fast to our confession and testimony of him. Where is your testimony?

Enter His Gates

Psalms 100: 1-5 (KJV)

1 Make a joyful noise unto the Lord, all ye lands.

2 Serve the Lord with gladness: come before his presence with singing.

3 Know ye that the Lord he is God: it is he that hath made us, and not we ourselves; we are his people, and the sheep of his pasture.

4 Enter into his gates with thanksgiving, and into his courts with praise: be thankful unto him, and bless his name.

5 For the Lord are good; his mercy is everlasting; and his truth endured to all generations.

The early church knew how to praise and worship God in

the beauty of holiness grateful hearts before the Lord. In everything we should give thanks appreciating who he is and the creator of the universe, awesome worship in his presence will manifest his presence far he is Holy.

Psalms 29:2 (KJV)

2 Give unto the Lord the glory due unto his name; worship the Lord in the beauty of holiness.

Psalms 150: 1-6 (KJV)

1 Praise ye the Lord. Praise God in the firmament of his power.

2 Praise him for his mighty acts: praise him according to his excellent greatness.

3 Praise him with the sound of the trumpet: praise him with the psaltery and harp.

4 Praise him with the timbrel and dance: praise him with stringed instruments and organs.

5 Praise him upon the loud cymbals: praise him upon the high sounding cymbals.

6 Let everything that hath breath praise the Lord. Praise you the Lord.

The Purpose of Our Praise

The purpose of our praise and worship is to glorify, honor, praise, exalt, and to please our God. Our worship must show adoration and loyalty to God for his grace in providing us with the way to escape the bondage of sin so we can have the salvation he so much wants to give us.

Establish Who God Is:

(1) Justice- God will make everything alright when mistreated his nature is a justice nature.

(2) Good-ness- God is good all the time even when we don't deserve, all the time God is good.

(3) Holiness- God is Holy, what does that mean (He is righteous, pure, clean) his majesty is always right prefect and moral (absolutely) no sin, or evil Holy is the Lord.

(4) Love- God is love he is light in him there is no darkness, his love is unexplainable.

(5) Sovereign- He rules, meaning he does whatever he wants to no one tell him what or how to do things. He can't be bought or manipulated God is in complete control of everything what ever happen well or bad he is God. Those are some of the characteristic of God just to name a few there is an atmosphere that is set when we enter into his presence.

Oh! Bless the Lord: oh my soul and all that is in me bless his holy name let the church say amen. The early church had this set in order of service this type of praise and worship set the atmosphere for the word of God. It was heartfelt was a ushering in of the Holy Spirit.

The Work of the Holy Spirit

The early church knew how to usher in the Holy Spirit.

Acts 1: 8 (KJV)

8 But ye shall receive power, after that the Holy Ghost is come upon you: and ye shall be witnesses unto me both in Jerusalem, and in all Judaea, and in Samaria, and unto the uttermost part of the earth.

The church today is so sleepy that some of us have fallen behind the Old Testament saints in our appropriation of what the spirit has to give. These are the days of Pentecost.

Joel 2:28 (KJV)

28 And it shall come to pass afterward, that I will pour out my spirit upon all flesh; and your sons and daughters shall prophesy, your old men shall dream dreams, your young men shall see visions:

The Holy Spirit is from Genesis to Revelations, he was working in the beginning.

Genesis 1:26 (KJV)

26 And God said; Let us make man in our image, after our likeness: and let them have dominion over the fish of the sea, and over the fowl of the air and over the cattle, and over all the earth, and over every creeping thing that crept upon the earth.

God said let us make man, who was God talking to?

Genesis 1:1-2 (KJV)

1 In the beginning God created the heavens and earth

2 And the earth was without form, and void; and darkness was upon the face or the deep. And the Spirit of God moved upon the face of the waters.

God created man in his own imagine God is a spirit the imagine of man the real person is a spirit, but when the Holy Spirit of God come into our heart he shed light on the darkness that was In man. The Holy Spirit reproduces Jesus on the inside. He is the third person of the God head. Now after the Pentecost experience we are a church (people) built on the foundation of the prophets and apostle to continue the work that church begun.

1st Peter 2:9 (NIV)

9 But ye are a chosen people a royal priesthood, a holy nation, God's special possession, that you may declare the praise of him who called you out of darkness into his wonderful light.

Sanctification

The work of the Holy Spirit in enabling believers to lead holy lives dedicated to service of God and conformed to his likeness.

Luke 3:16

16 He shall baptize with the Holy Ghost and fire.

1st Peter 1:2 (KJV)

2 Fire implies the Holy Spirit's works of purification and judgment sanctification is a special work of the Holy Spirit.

Romans 14:17 (KJV)

17 He requires believers to be sanctified it is a necessary part of being a Christian. The Holy Spirit produces sanctification.

The Process of Sanctification

2nd Corinthians 3:18 (KJV)

But we all with open faces beholding as in a glass the glory of the Lord are changed into the same image from glory of the Lord, are changed into the same image from glory to glory, even as by the Spirit of the Lord. A process of God by grace by which the believer is separated from sin, purified by a live lived in the spirit

Romans 8:1-4 (KJV)

1 There is therefore now no condemnation to them which are in Christ Jesus, who walk not after the flesh, but after the Spirit.

2 For the law of the Spirit of life in Christ Jesus hath made me free from the law of sin and death.

3 For what the law could not do, in that it was weak through

the flesh, God sending his own Son in the likeness of sinful flesh, and for sin, condemned sin in the flesh:

4 That the righteousness of the law might be fulfilled in us, who walk not after the flesh, but after the Spirit.

The Spirit of Adoption

A life set a part for the master's use or purpose to make Holy.

In the process the believer has to submit to God's will, resisting sin, seeking holiness and working to be more Godly. God's grace is now on the inside where we were once under the Moses law from the outside the law has moved to the inside so there is no longer an excuse to sin because of grace.

Romans 6:1-2 (KJV)

1 What shall we say then?

Shall we continue in sin, that grace may abound?

2 God forbid. How shall we, that are dead to sin, live any longer therein?

To seek to sin continually and use God's grace to excuse it later is to trample the blood of Christ underfoot Hebrew 10:29.

Lest embrace our sanctification it is our inheritance in Jesus Christ.

He sent the Holy Ghost down here so he could help us in our walks and divine destinies with him.

Direct Contact with the Holy Spirit

1. Will draw the unsaved sinner to Jesus
2. Will convict both unbelievers and believers
3. Will regenerate our human spirits
4. Will draw us closer to the Lord
5. Will sanctify us in the Lord
6. Will help us with our prayer life
7. Will guide us into all truth
8. Will teach us all things
9. Will anoint us with his divine power
10. Will be our helper and comforter in this life
11. The 9 gifts of the Holy Spirit
12. The 9 fruits of the Holy Spirit

Communion- (2nd Corinthians 13:14) KJV

14 The grace of the Lord Jesus Christ, and the love of God, and the communion of the Holy Ghost, is with you all. Amen.

Fellowship- (Philippians 2:1) KJV

1 If there be therefore any consolation in Christ, if any comfort of love, if any fellowship of the Spirit, if any bowels and mercies.

Walk In the Spirit- (Galatians 5:25) KJV

25 If we live in the Spirit, let us also walk in the Spirit

Every Christian needs to learn how to walk in the Holy Spirit.

The Sanctification Process by the Word and the Holy Spirit

(Redemption, righteousness, and sanctification)

We have to work out our salvation with fear and trembling.

(Set us apart) unto himself and to transform us into becoming more holy instruments of righteous for his use.

(A) The state of growing in divine grace

(B) To set apart for holy purpose

(C) The process of being made holy resulting in a changed lifestyle for the believers.

Chapter 13
To Live a Godly Life

We should be grateful to our Heavenly Father for he has love for us unconditional we have all we need to live the life pertaining to Godliness.

He has given:

(1) His son Jesus Christ (word)

(2) His blood

(3) His armor

(4) Testimony to overcome

(5) His name

(6) Praise and worship

(7) Dreams and vision (prophetic)

(8) Gifts of the spirit

(9) Fruits of the spirit

(10) The Holy Spirit

(11 Prophecy

How awesome is he? God has covered all things for his children once we get in position study, pay attention to the road map, instructions, we will do ourselves justice. No one told me I inherited an enemy who want to see me fail; no one took the time to teach me as a babe, once you get tired of being sick and tired and say enough is enough. Go into the world and preach the Gospel to every creature because Jesus is on his way back for a people he got you covered.

In School

In school is a time in your life when it is shaped, sometimes even transformed. I remember when I let God really begin to teach me the things and mystery of his kingdom. I was working for a big company called U.S. Support making $12.00 an hour I worked 12 to 14 hours a day. God begin to speak to me not only through his word, but through dreams and visions. God visits us through dreams he pull me off that job. I begin to learn and understand kingdom principles.

Roman 12:2 (KJV)

2 And be not conformed to this world, but be ye transformed by the renewing of your mind; that ye may prove what is good and acceptable and perfect will of God.

Kingdom principles and economic is not like the worlds principle and economic. But God school of learning is a life journey. In a dream I saw myself in school going from one class to another I was/am in school learning the ways of God.

Matthew 6:33 (KJV)

33 But seek ye first the kingdom of God, and his righteousness; and all these things shall be added unto you.

Let us think kingdom life. I believe God build character first, we can only be trusted to steward that which we have the character to maintain. God will not give more if we fail to steward what we already have for kingdom purpose. We have to learn in school to depend on God's economic system and not man economic system. God gives responsibilities to us to succeed in our purpose all things comes from God and fulfilling our kingdom purpose depends on accepting God's mandate to be as. In this lesson he would say the Jesus (word) on the inside of you must grow in order from that word to grow (mature) is to correct with the word in the scriptures, we need to grow in him more on to maturity. That is why it is Important to feed on the word of God daily because Jesus (the word) needs to be fed daily. He is the Word of God. Let us cross over to the other side and grow in Christ Jesus to a perfect man in him. Spiritual growth is a lifelong process that depends on our study and application of God's Word and our walk in the spirit.

Revelation

2nd Corinthians 2:9 (NIV)

9 But he said to me, "My grace is sufficient for you, for my power is made perfect in weakness."

I remember when I was working at a certain place it was a warehouse where I had to stand on my feet for hours one day my feet begin to swell from so much standing, then it hit me two big fat feet. I was unable to go to work for three days, I begin to panic God what am I going to do?" I asked? Why now I need this job rent is due, car insurance due my bills are due, and Lord help me! I cried! He said my grace is sufficient for you my strength are made strong in your weakness. How the Apostle Paul must have felt when this word came a "RHEMA WORD" from God. God I asked what exactly does that mean for me even though this is in your word, what does that mean? And the Lord said, "In your weakness I can work through you my power, my strength, my anointing even though you are weak in this area of your life I need you to give your weakness unto me and let me prove who I am in your life and this is for my glory. What a revelation for me and for you, God is saying he need you to give him all of your weakness and faults so he can make himself strong in your infirmities. God do not need our strength he need all of our weakness so he can show himself through you. I begin to give him all of my weakness so God would be glorified in my life; our strength is in completion with God. Give him your weakness he wants them all.

Pick up your cross and follow him daily the more I love Jesus and pursue him with my whole undivided heart, my entire soul every fiber of my strength and every area of my mind- the mire grace is visible to me and experience by me.

Pray that God's grace be enough for you in your weakness, pray that the change come the spirit and the bride say come.

Anointed For Greatness

Anoint means "to smear or rub with oil and implication, to consecrate for office or religious service"

Anointed for a special purpose- To be a builder; to be a writer, to be a teacher, to be a wife, leader, to be a mother. It is only God who can anoint a person for a specific purpose; oil was used to symbolize what God is doing. Jesus Christ was anointed by God with the Holy Spirit to spread the good news and free those who have been held captive by sin. Luke 4:18. Jesus ascended to heaven and gave the gift of the Holy Spirit to his bride. Now all his followers are anointed, chosen for a specific purpose in furthering God's Kingdom.

2nd Corinthians 1:21-22 (KJV)

21 Now he who establishes us with you in Christ and hath anointed us is God;

22 Who hath also has sealed us, and given the earnest of the Sprit in our hearts.

It is the anointed that destroy every yoke in our life and enable us to do what God has plan and purpose inside of you.

Jeremiah 1:5 (KJV)

5 Before I formed thee in the belly I knew thee, and before thou came forth out of the womb I sanctified thee, and I ordained thee a prophet unto the nations.

Born and anointed for greatness we have a problem in the body with identity knowing who we are in him. Even though God called Jeremiah to be a prophet to speak for him he also was a writer. Once we cross over from our religion or religious setting. There is an identity crisis in the body of Christ. The early church knew who they were in the body of Christ they grew in him.

Spiritual Growth

This is a process of becoming more like Jesus, the Holy Spirit begin the process of making us more like him conforming us to the image our goal in him is spiritual growth not religion. What we need for spiritual growth comes "through our knowledge of him, which is the key to obtaining ever thing we need in and from him.

2nd Peter 1:3-8 (KJV)

3 According as his divine power hath given unto us all things that pertain unto life and godliness, through the knowledge of him that hath called us to glory and virtue:

4 Whereby are given unto us exceeding great and precious promises: that by these ye might be partakers of the divine nature, having escaped the corruption that is in the world through lust.

5 And beside this giving all diligence, add to your faith virtue; and to virtue knowledge;

6 And to knowledge temperance; and to temperance patience; and to patience godliness;

7 And to godliness brotherly kindness; and to brotherly kindness charity.

8 For if these things be in you, and abound, they make you that ye shall neither be barren nor unfruitful in the knowledge of our Lord Jesus Christ.

When the transformation of salvation takes place spiritual growth begins in 2nd Corinthians 5:17 tells us Therefore if any man be in Christ, he is a new creature: old things are passed away; behold all things are become new.

The Holy Spirit showed me a simple growth process of growing in Christ; once we are born again we exchange life with Christ his life comes to live in us our life he takes; now the baby Jesus is inside of you Jesus is the word.

John 1:1-2 (KJV)

1 In the beginning was the Word, and the Word was with God, and the Word was God.

2 The same was in the beginning with God.

Kingdom Economics

The Kingdom of God is God's rule and reign, and when we surrender our life to God we enter into the kingdom. It is the self-sacrifice God is in the business of giving to others a living sacrifice.

Romans 12:1

1 I beseech you therefore, brethren by the mercies of God, that ye present your bodies a living sacrifice, holy, acceptable unto God, which is your reasonable service.

Kingdom economic is not a "get rich" scheme, but rather a system of providing for people needs as they need it we have been transformed out of darkness into his marvelous light to do kingdom work to handle the family business, ask God for divine connection. Kingdom economic begins to flow as we are divinely inter- connected; attached to one another. We see this corporate dynamic operational in early church testimony.

Acts 4:32-35 (NKJV)

32 Now the multitude of those who believed were of one heart and one soul; neither did anyone say that any of the things he possessed was his own, but they had all things in common. 33 And with great power the apostles gave witness to the resurrection of the Lord Jesus and great grace was upon them all. 34 Nor was there anyone among them who lacked; for all who were possessors of lands or houses sold them, and brought the proceeds of the things that were sold, 35 and laid them at the apostles' feet; and they distributed to each as anyone had need.

Kingdom economic working together in partnership with God in his Kingdom. Amen

Two Kingdoms

Our attitude should be the same as Christ Jesus in the kingdom. Jesus went about preaching the gospel of the kingdom everywhere he went.

There is over one hundred and fifty reference Jesus made to the "Kingdom" in the new testimony when he taught us how to pray. He included the phrase "Thy Kingdom Come." He went about preaching the gospel of the kingdom.

Matthew 4:8-9 (KJV)

8 Again, the devil take him up into an exceeding high mountain, and showed him all the kingdoms of the world, and the glory of them;

9 And said unto him, all these things will I give thee, if thou wilt fall down and worship me.

Is Satan able to give these kingdoms of the world to Jesus? Satan is referred to the as the God of the world. There is a system that is of this world an order of things of this world.

Kingdom Conflict

Know that these two kingdoms are in conflict with each other. The world view is the drive to succeed at any cost, corruption, manipulation of clients, greed, selfish ambitious, self-promotion and self, we need to get back to spiritual roots of Biblical property so that we can learn how to operate from a kingdom builder should be just as Jesus did preach and teach the good news of Jesus Christ. Jesus is the way to the Kingdom of Heaven

Chapter 14
The Word of God

Psalms 133:119 (KJV)

119 Order my steps in thy word: and let not any iniquity have dominion over me.

We want the Lord to order our steps on a daily basis. I love the word of God we can take this word apply it to our life, situation and circumstance. Jesus is the living word that lives on the inside of us as we meditate, and feed ourselves daily he (the word) will grow on the inside of us oh! What a wonderful and awesome God we serve as he changes us from image to image from glory to glory through his wonderful word.

The Milk of the Word

Like newborn babies, desire (crave) pure milk of the word, so that by it you may grow in respect to salvation. 1st Peter 2:2 (KJV)

"In understanding how to grow as a disciple of Jesus Christ"

He goes on to say if so be ye have tasted that the Lord is (good) gracious.

The sincere milk of the word is a must in order for us to grow. There is no substitute for reading the word of God to grow in our faith walk. This is called True Spiritual Walk. We get the knowledge of Jesus through the reading of the word Jesus is the word made flesh.

John 1:1; 14 (KJV)

1 In the beginning was the Word, and the Word was with God, and the Word was God.

14 The Word became flesh and made his dwelling among us. We have seen his glory, the glory of the one and only Son, who came from the Father, full of grace and truth.

So the milk of the word would be Jesus (Baby Jesus) in you so if the Baby Jesus in you needs to grow Jesus (the word) will need milk and nourishment to become strong and mature just as a new born baby need milk to grow.

The sincere milk can be defined as the word of God to the babe who is a true believer and disciple (learning) of Jesus Christ (the word) Gods word is the very source that we need from the pages of the bible in order for the babe to grow, without deception, defilement, error or any other interference. This is also a way to have defense against false teachers.

The word of God teaches there will be many false prophets (teachers) in the last days and he encourage us in his word to desire the sincere milk of the word these false teachers are on a mission to over throw our faith to cause us not to grow. To read the word of God is a command from our Lord this is putting our faith in him to practice. Don't worry about trying to understand his word all at once he gives little by little. Line upon line and precept upon precept here or little and there a little.

2nd Peter 1:19-21 (JKV)

19 We have also a more sure word of prophecy; whereunto ye do well that ye take heed, as unto a light that shine in a dark place, until the day dawn, and the day star arise in your hearts:

20 Knowing this first that no prophecy of the scripture is of any private interpretation.

21 For the prophecy came not in old time by the will of man: but holy men of God spoke as they were moved by the Holy Ghost.

We are first and foremost disciples (leaders) we must first desire get the milk of the word so we can make disciples of all nations.

Joshua 1:8 (JKV]

8 This book of the law shall not depart out of thy mouth; but thou shall meditate therein day and night, that thou may observe to do according to all that is written therein: for then thou shall make thy way prosperous, and then thou shall have good success.

The milk of the word is the good news the gospel of Jesus Christ his death, burial, and resurrection. Get the milk of the word.

The Bread

Now we came to the bread Jesus declare, I am the Bread of Life.

Matthew 4:3-4 (JKV)

3 And when the tempter came to him, he said; "if thou be the Son of God, command that these stones be made bread."

4 Bur he answered and said, it is written, Man shall not live by bread alone, but by every word that proceed out of the

mouth of God. John 6:35 (JKV) I Am The Bread Of Life.

Jesus had fed the people so they were looking for him they were full. Jesus told them you seek me for a sign and he (Jesus) told them to believe and they will have life he is the bread of life. Ask yourself these questions

1. If we are shown a sign, what are we going to do?
2. What are the works that God wants us to do?

Jesus answered "The work God wants is this: that you believe in the one whom God sent" that's the work God wants: "Believe in the one whom God has sent" Jesus is saying develop a relationship with the living God fellowship with him, minister to him, praise and worship him, come to know the true and living God he is the one who gives manna from heaven. Jesus say I am the bread of life whoever comes to me shall never be hungry, who believes in me shall never be thirsty. Blessed are those who seek after righteousness for they shall be filled. The bread that comes down from heaven I the bread that feeds our spirits, soul but not our bodies. Oh taste and see that the Lord he is good. The father feed his children as a father feed his children. The Israelites had to depend on God every day for the provision (bread) we partake of Christ body the bread of life even in the bread of the Lord's Supper. After the resurrection, Jesus eating the bread with his disciples was a token of his victory over death (Luke 24:30 JKV). And the Christians after that meet on the first day of the week for the breaking of bread (Acts 20:7 JKV).

The Meat of the Word

Moving on from the milk, to the bread, from the bread to the meat of the word. There are some in the body of Christ that should be teachers of the word of God, but because of the spiritual growth and misleading the word has not grown on the inside it is a spiritual development in as spiritual retardation.

Hebrews 5:11-14 (KJV)

11 Of whom we have many things to say and hard to be uttered, seeing you are dull of hearing.

12 For when the time ye ought to be teachers, ye have need that one teach you again which be the first principles of the oracles of God; and are become such as have need of milk, and not strong meat.

13 For everyone that use milk is unskilled in the word of righteousness: for he is a babe.

14 But strong meat belongs to them that are of full age, even those who by reason of the use have their senses exercised to discern both good and evil.

Leaving the basic foundation going on to stronger foundation (meat of the word) spiritual growth. Being a Christian means moving forward from starting out as a babe and going onto full maturity.

Matthew 5:48 (JKV)

48 Be ye therefore perfect, even as your Father which is in heaven is perfect.

Away pick up your word, pray ask God to give you knowledge wisdom and revelation of his word. Ask him to open your spiritual understanding.

Paul wrote to the Hebrews and told them not to let the root of bitterness spring up in their heart and minds (Hebrews 12:15 JKV)

The Root of Bitterness

Rebellion- Outward

This root that is in the heart comes and shows up on the outside because of REBELLION it causes:

(1) Hatred

(2) Resentment

(3) Violence

(4) Un-Forgiveness

(5) Murder

(6) Anger

(7) Retaliation

(8) Memory Recall

(9) Pride

(10) Un-Teachable

Rejection- Inward

Rejection comes from this root of bitterness from within

(1) Un-Fairness

(2) Withdrawal

(3) Pouting

(4) Fantasy

(5) Vivid Imagination

(6) Loneliness

(7) Talk-nests

(8) Fears

(9) Lust

(10) Insecurity

The root of bitterness will hinder a believer's relationship with the Lord and service to him. Bitterness open the door to the enemy also effect people physically keep them sick. I am a root that is deadly to us the only way to remove bitterness is forgiveness. Jesus tells us to forgive our brother daily. Peter asked Lord how many times should I forgive my brother who sins against me Jesus say 70x7, but he went on to say as many times as he sin against you even if it is more we should forgive. We are to be strong in the Lord and in the power of his might, put on the whole armor of God. It is if great important to study or word for growth. We should read, study, understand, comprehend and apply strong meat belongs to full age mature Christian.

Identification in Him

Ephesians 1:16-19 (JKV)

16. I cease not to give thanks for you, making mention of you in my prayers;

17 That the God of our Lord Jesus Christ, the Father of glory, may give unto you the Spirit of Wisdom and Revelation in the Knowledge of him:

18 The eyes of your understanding being enlightened; that ye may know what the hope of his calling is, and what the riches of the glory of his inheritance in the saints,

19 And what is the exceeding greatness of his power to us-ward who believes, according to the working of his mighty power.

    The early church did not have the problems that we have today with the many different concepts taught within the body of Christ. The first century apostles had been taught by Christ himself and they believed the same thing they set the foundation for the church, the doctrine of the gospel of Jesus Christ. We are to take up were they left off the foundation has already been laid.

Ephesians 2:19-21 (KJV)

19 Now therefore ye are no mire strangers and foreigners, but fellow citizens with the saints, and of the household of God;

20 And are built upon the foundation of the apostles and prophets, Jesus Christ himself being the chief corner stone;

21 In whom all the building fitly framed together growth unto a holy temple in the Lord:

Getting back to the basic and order of service without the Holy Spirit we will accomplish little and without the prophetic we will accomplish little there are many doctrines and a church on every corner, but few are operating under the direction of the Holy Spirit. Return unto me says the Lord and I will return unto you. I see among believers and no word? Why so much prediction from human flesh? Imagination of their heart   the Holy Spirit is not allowed to work in our mist quench not the Holy Spirit the church knew how to wait on the Lord.

The Mystery of the Church

In Paul's writing about the mystery of the church mean the secret of the church being revealed. God have hidden the mystery (secret) of his church now he reveals it to his prophets and apostles. The New Testament Church the Body of Christ Jesus. The gentiles are one with the Jews making up his body and in the church there are neither Jews nor Greek, a Barbarian, bond, nor free, male neither, female all are one in Christ this is one of the glorious mystery that is being revealed to all believers in Christ.

Ephesians 5:25-27 (KJV)

25 Husbands, love your wives, even as Christ also loved the church, and gave himself for it;

26 That he might sanctify and cleanse it with the washing of water by the word,

27 That he might present it to himself a glorious church, not having spot, or wrinkle, or any such thing; but that it should be holy and without blemish.

The church belongs to Jesus Christ the real true church the body of the blood bought born again believers. Jesus is the head not man praise the name of Jesus. The first mention of the church by Jesus is in the book of Matthew 16:13-18 (KJV)

13 When Jesus came into the coasts of Caesarea Philippi, he asked his disciples, saying, who do men say that I the Son of man am?

14 And they said, some say that thou art John the Baptist: some, Elias; and others, Jeremiah, or one of the prophets.

15 He said unto them, But who say ye that I am?

16 And Simon Peter answered and said, Thou art the Christ, the Son of the living God.

17 And Jesus answered and said into him, Blessed art thou, Simon Barjona, for flesh and blood hath not revealed it unto thee, but my Father which is in heaven.

18 And I say also say unto thee, that thou art Peter, and upon this rock I will build my church; and the gates of hell shall not prevail against it.

The church is his church (Jesus) he is the builder of it. That's why we shouldn't get offended when people put us out of their buildings, because born again believer belongs to the body of Christ. "Jesus has purchased the church with his own blood it is his church". Upon this Rock Jesus is that Rock.

The body of believers is the true church of Jesus Christ his blood bought body washed in the blood of the Lamb.

Where ever there are two are more gather together in his name he is in the mist lifting up that wonderful name of Jesus.

There are so many churches and denominations but the true church his bride is his body of believers.

Many will come in my name saying I am the Christ the Antichrist is on the rise.

Jesus our High Priest

Hebrews 4:14 (JKV)

14 Seeing then that we have a great high priest that is passed into the heavens, Jesus the Son of God, let us hold fast our profession.

Jesus is our resting places those of us who belongs to Jesus. Aren't you glad Jesus gives us rest?

Matthew 11:28-30 (KJV)

"28 come to me, all you who are weary and burdened, and I will give you rest.

29 Take my yoke upon you and learn from me, for I am gentle and humble in heart, and you will find rest for your souls.

30 For my yoke is easy and my burden is light."

His rest is deep, peaceful, safe and everlasting. His rest which develops into heaven and he gives to us daily Jesus our high priest. He is forever making intercession for his church (people).

Hebrews 4:15-16 (KJV)

15 For we do not have a high priest which cannot be touched with the feeling of our infirmities; but was in all points tempted like as we are yet without sin.

16 Let us therefore come boldly unto the throne of grace that we may obtain mercy, and find grace to help in time of need.

The throne of Christ today our high priest until the end of age is an intercessory throne Christ is ruling by intercession. In prayer we contend, wrestle, fight, agonize and this very serious warfare. Christian life and service is seen as warfare

Travailing Prayer

When God put burden heaviness on our heart we begin to travail, moan, groan, and cry out in the power of the Holy Spirit.

Laboring in the spirit as a woman labor to bring forth a child a pushing a birthing sometimes this takes place days, weeks, months. Travail a state of pregnancy from the onset of labor to the birth of a child.

The apostle Paul did travail on behalf of others (in the spirit) until the spirit of Christ was formed on those whom God had placed on his heart. So did the early church they gather together for prayer and the breaking of bread (the word of God). It is mantle of prayer lead by the Holy Spirit to pray for the burden of the Lord. Spiritual travail is a level of intensity marked by the Holy Spirit to bring the burden to pass through prayer a given promise a prophetic insight or a Holy Spirit illuminated need in a person, church, city or nation a birthing in the spirit.

Prayer Warfare

From travailing to prevailing prayer warfare is said to be the seventh and highest level of prevailing prayer. It's the prolonged, intensified form of prevailing prayer focused on defeating and routing Satan so that Christ will be done and his kingdom advanced. Prayer warfare is fought individually and collectively. Requires constant alertness and readiness and coordinated by the Holy Spirit. We make the proclamations, decrees, declarations, orders, instructions and directives by God's leading to entitles principalities and power, forces, domains, governments, authorities above and below, people and objects to adjust, turn and respond of God's divine order and manifestation.

The Holy Spirit: who empowers us to pray, gives us what to pray about and then the right precise prayed language. Prevailing prayer our most militant prayer language, we are a church on the move to restore back to the Kingdom power, authority, dominion to our Lord and Savior Jesus Christ who will reign and rule forever and ever

Chapter 15
Pruning Time

John 15:1-2 (KJV)

1 I am the true vine, and my Father is the husbandman.

2 Every branch in me that bear not fruit he takes away: and every branch that bear fruit he purge it, that it may bring forth more fruit.

How God Prunes Us?

God prunes us through his word his word remove unwanted branches.

Hebrews 4:12 (KJV)

12 For the word of God is quick, and powerful, and sharper than any two-edged sword, piercing even to the dividing asunder of soul and spirit, and of the joints and marrow, and is a discerner of the thoughts and intents of the heart.

Even Jesus was prune "He (Jesus) learned obedience through the things he suffered" Sometimes pruning involves trials we have to be cleanse by the washing of the water of the word in order to service and minister to God and to his people. There must be purify in the priesthood it is through this pruning process that God makes and mold us to stand before him in holiness unto him.

Listening To God

Learning to listen to God was a struggle for me, but I was determining to hear God for myself after all I went through when I first came into the Kingdom and knowledge of our Lord and Savior Jesus Christ. There was

It is much distraction from inside out of the church. #1 Instead of people wanted you to serve the God who create and save you they wanted me to worship and serve them.

Instead of discipline me there were other things and actives going on. I learned if one is not equipped and called to do certain things in the church it is hard to do. Learning to listen to God was a hard task for me because I didn't know how to trust God as my heavenly father, but God was patient with me through it all. It took me year and years. Sometimes I would give up and go right back to Egypt (the world).

James 1:22-25 (KJV)

22 Be ye doers of the word, and not hearers only, deceiving your own selves.

23 For any be a hearer of the word, and not a doer, he is like unto a man beholding his natural face in a glass.

24 For he behold himself, and go his way, and straightway forgotten what manner of man he was.

25 But whoso look into the perfect law of liberty, and continue therein, he being not a forgetful hearer, but a doer of the work, this man shall be blessed in his deed.

God not only speak through his word, God speaks through

dreams, vision, people, and children nature. God in his awesome have many ways to speak, but with me I found he speaks through his word, dreams and vision God will meet you where you are whatever level you are on through your personality and prayer.

The Operation of the Gifts of the Spirit

1st John 2:20 (KJV)

20 But ye have unction from the Holy One, and ye know all things.

In chapter 9, I explained the gifts of the prophetic that Jesus gifts to his body the gifts of apostle, prophets, evangelist, pastors and teachers.

Now we come to the gifts that the Holy Spirit gives in the church (Body) of Christ.

Revelations Gifts

1. The word of wisdom

2. The word of knowledge

3. Discerning of Spirits

These are what we call supplemental gifts meaning these are used to build up church the manifestation of these gifts are sign that one is filled with the Holy Spirit of God, but we do have to test the spirit everything God use for his people the devil copy it.

Power Gifts	Vocal Gifts
4. Gifts of healing	7. Prophecy
5. Working of miracles	8. Kind of tongues
6 Gifts of faith Interpretations	9.Tongues and

1st Corinthians 12:7 (KJV)

7 But the manifestation of the Spirit is given to every man to profit withal.

These gifts was in operation in the early church Paul writing to the Corinthians to give order in the church to admonish them to do things decent and in order the way God design for his church to operate. It would take another whole book to discuss each gift that the Holy Spirit gives to operate in the body. It is under the anointing of the Holy Spirit under his lead. The anointing of God means to be set aside for service set apart for God use.

Then Samuel took a flask of oil and poured it on his head, and kissed him and said it is not because the Lord has anointed you commander over his inheritance?

1st Samuel 16:13-14 (KJV)

13 Then Samuel took the horn of oil, and anointed him in the midst of his brethren: and the Spirit of the Lord came upon David from that day forward. So Samuel rose up, and went to Ramah.

14 But the Spirit of the Lord departed from Saul, and an evil spirit from the Lord troubled him.

This was because Saul was disobedience of God. It is a terrible thing to fall in the hand of an angry God. If you are anointed by God embrace that anointing watch over it, protect the anointing it is a very precious gift from him.

2nd Corinthians 1:21 (KJV)

21 Now he which establishes us with you in Christ, and hath anointed us, is God;

How does this happen? It happen by truly being born again, Jesus answered and said to him.

John 3:3 (KJV)

3 Jesus answered and said unto him Verily, verily, I say unto thee, except a man be born again, he cannot see the kingdom of God.

We become priests and kings, God will anoint us, yes he will anoint for service unto him.

Baptized With the Holy Spirit

Acts 2:1-4 (KJV)

1 And when the day of Pentecost was fully come, they were all with one accord in one place.

2 And suddenly there came a sound from heaven as of a rushing mighty wind, and it filled the entire house where they were sitting.

3 And there appeared unto them cloven tongues like as of fire, and it sat upon each of them.

4 And they were all filled with the Holy Ghost, and began to speak with other tongues, as the Spirit gave them utterance.

Just as the anointing oil was poured on the head of Aaron and over his beard, so we can feel the anointing oil of the Holy Spirit as he moves upon us. It is the anointing that breaks and destroy every yoke.

This is the way of God order of service for his people it is time for the church to get back and return to Gods order and pattern of service let's do it Gods way. By the word of God, praise and worship, salvation, healing and deliverance from demons, testimony, preaching the word gifts of the Holy Spirit, repentance, true heart repentance will change the heart and mind of Gods people.

Empowered To Rule and Reign

Through Christ we are empowered to rule and reign because

of his precious blood we are in the kingdom of God which is his people, bride, and church. We have an inheritance in him; we have been given the keys to the kingdom of heaven. The authority to bind and loose, the key of knowledge, wisdom and understanding the mysteries of the kingdom.

Revelation 3:7-8 (JKV)

7 And to the angel of the church in Philadelphia write; these things said he that is holy, he that is true, he that hath the key of David, he that opens, and no man shuts; and shuts, and no man opens.

8 I know thy works: behold, I have set before thee an open door, and no man can shut it: for thou hast a little strength, and hast kept my word, and hast not denied my name.

All who are true believers in Christ have the truth (the key) to admit others into the kingdom, because they pass this truth on in the power and authority of the Holy Spirit. God is a God of truth and he is always moving.

Jesus is the door he is the only way to the father coming any other way is the wrong door.

John 10:1-3 (KJV)

1 Verily, verily, I say unto you, He that enters not by the door into the sheepfold, but climb up some other way, the same is a thief and a robber.

2 But he that enters in by the door is the shepherd of the sheep.

Use Your Key (s)

Everyone has a key in the kingdom if God to the door. The key is prayer use you key. We are in transition from one era to another from the Holy place of service to God to the Holy of Holies of being intimate moving into the mystery of a bride (marriage) where God inhabits fellowship with his people as his Shekinah Glory is restored in the temple of his people.

Psalms 24:9 (KJV)

9 Lift up your heads, O ye gates; even lift them up, ye everlasting doors; and the King of glory shall come in.

Child of God keys are used to lock and unlock doors.

Matthew 23:13 (KJV)

13 But woe unto you, scribes and Pharisees, hypocrites! For ye shut up the kingdom of heaven against men: for ye neither go in yourselves, neither suffer ye them that are entering to go in.

The gospel of Jesus Christ is a key to the kingdom. Jesus also talked about gates. The key belongs to all born again blood washed believers by faith only through our Lord and Savior Jesus Christ Amen.

John 10:3 (KJV)

3 To him the porter opens; and the sheep hear his voice: and he calls his own sheep by name, and lead them out.

The porter is the door keeper who is the Holy Spirit yes we can use our keys.

Seek Him with Your Whole Heart

If we seek God with our whole heart with holding nothing from him, asking for him to show us the promise he will show up.

Hebrews 11:1 (KJV)

1 Now faith is the substance of things hoped for, the evidence of things not seen.

(P.U.S.H.) pray until something happens seek and you shall find, ask and it shall be given to you, knock and the door shall be open unto you Jesus talk a lots about faith little faith, no faith, and great faith.

Since faith is one of the gifts of the spirit and faith is included in our armor then our faith should grow to the extent we should be like the woman who went before the unjust judge she said avenges me of my adversary.

He would not at first, but she didn't give up she was persistent in her plea to the judge. He said, thou he did not fear God or man he was tired of the little old persistent lady everyday worrying him, we can learn from this lesson if we just keep pushing, P.U.S.H.

I understand faith is a process that turns desires to hope and hope into reality. Seek him with your whole heart; seek him why he may be found. Through faith we receive the promises.

Hebrews 6:11-12 (KJV)

11 And we desire that every one of you do show the same diligence to the full assurance of hope unto the end:

12 That ye be not slothful, but followers of them who through faith and patience inherit the promises.

Romans 10:17 (KJV)

17 So then faith cometh by hearing, and hearing by the word of God.

This is why it is so important to spend time alone with God reading the word. So our faith can grow and come alive. And we know our faith take time, there will be no shortcuts but know this our God do not respond to part-time seekers; seek him with your whole heart meditate on him day and night.

Joshua 1:8 (KJV)

This book of the law shall not depart out of thy mouth; but thou shall mediate therein day and night, that thou may observe to do according to all that is written therein: for then thou shall make thy way prosperous, and then thou shall have good success.

By faith push, by the word push! Seek him with your whole heart.

Overcomes

raying in the spirit, and using the word of God, because we have a real enemy that we cannot see we need spiritual weapons to defeat our foe. Solider on the front line we are a militant church and the battle belongs to the Lord. In him, through him, for him, unto him we can do all things through Christ who strengthen us Philippians 4:13.

Our prayer and the word are powerful weapons against our enemies. Sharpen your sword more than a conquer threw Christ Jesus. Be an overcome our faith and patient will be tested I tell you that "men always ought to pray and not lose heart (faint)".

Philippians 4:6 (KJV)

6 Be careful for nothing; but in everything by prayer and supplication with thanksgiving let your requests be made known unto God.

Romans 8:26-27 (KJV)

26 Likewise the Spirit also helpeth our infirmities: for we know not what we should pray for as we ought: but the Spirit itself make intercession for us with groaning which cannot be uttered.

27 And he that searched the heart knows what is the mind of the Spirit he makes intercession for the saints according to the will of God.

Our God stands ready to provide us with the strength, wisdom and courage we need to stand against our enemy, but he wants us first to come before him boldly and ask pray his will be done in your life we are overcomes.

Chapter 16

The Wind

The early church was in agreement with one another they were all on one accord. In one place praying, singing, worshiping God. Praise and worship will always bring in the awesome spirit of God. The early church knew how to pray, praise and worship in spirit and in truth.

Acts 2:1-4 (KJV)

1 And when the day of Pentecost was fully come, they were all with one accord in one place.

2 And suddenly there came a sound from heaven as of a rushing mighty wind, and it filled the entire house where they were sitting.

3 And there appeared unto them cloven tongues like as of fire, and it sat upon each of them.

4 And they were all filled with the Holy Ghost, and began to speak with other tongues, as the Spirit gave them utterance.

The church had to depend totally of the Holy Ghost (Spirit) for healing, the word, prophecy, miracles etc.

The bible was not yet fully written now we have the word and the spirit. The Holy Spirit has many names one of his names is the wind. The Holy Spirit is a person third person of the trinity.

John 3:8 (KJV)

8 The wind blows where it will, and thou hear the sound thereof, but canst not tell whence it cometh, and whither it goes so is every one that is born of the Spirit.

To me this is supernatural the wind is invisible; we cannot see the source or the destination of the wind it is a mysterious unseen force. The wind is also a powerful force. The move (wind) of the spirit is God at work and the wind of the Holy Spirit is a mystery in the church. We need the wind of God to move in these last and evil days we need the wind. Stand in agreement with me in prayer, while we ask the Lord to send his wind like on the day of Pentecost. Let us pray for the mighty rushing wind.

This Is That

When the wind blows and God moves by his spirit I have seen people laugh in the spirit, get drunk or slain in the spirit. This is that.

Acts 2:14-17 (KJV)

14 But Peter, standing up with the eleven, lifted up his voice, and said unto them, Ye men of Judaea, and all ye that dwell at Jerusalem, be this known unto you, and hearken to my words:

15 For these are not drunken as ye suppose, (think) seeing it is but the third hour of the day.

16 But this is that which was spoken by the prophet Joel;

17 And it shall come to pass in the last days, said God; I

will pour out my Spirit upon all flesh: and your sons and your daughter shall prophesy, and your young men shall see visions, and your old men shall dream dreams:

This is that.

Here Comes the Bride

In the beginning of this book I talked about the fivefold ministry gifts. The Holy Spirit signifying how the church is to function with the fivefold ministry set in place. We may think we know, but we really don't know we have gotten so far away from how God set things in order, because some want to have a one man show and no more.

Ephesians 4:4-6 (KJV)

4 There are one body, and one Spirit, even as ye are called in one hope of your calling;

5 One Lord, one faith, one baptism,

6 One God and Father of all, who is above all, and through all, and in you all.

> One Body- The Body of Christ
>
> One Lord- Jesus Christ
>
> One Faith- Apostolic of the Apostles
>
> One Baptism- in Jesus Name (water and spirit)

The water baptism is a wonderful picture of Christ's death, burial and resurrection.

Romans 6:3 (KJV)

3 Know ye not, that so many of us as were baptized into Jesus Christ were baptized into his death?

Don't you know that all of us who were baptized into Christ Jesus were baptized into his death?

The spiritual baptism "into Christ" is performed by the Holy Spirit the moment a repentant sinner accepts the gift of salvation and is born again; our faith in the finished work of Christ saves.

Ephesians 2:8-9 (KJV)

8 For by grace are ye saved through (faith); and that not of yourselves: it is the gift of God:

9 Not of works let no man boast.

The body of Christ is his bride. We are members of one body not just a building we assemble in on certain nights are on Sundays or Saturdays whenever you assemble. The body consists of many members.

The real church blood brought, born again believers is this mystery which we seek. Christ loves his bride which is very, very special and that's why the New Testament goes to such length to present to us the identity and the uniqueness and whole theology of the church (bride of Christ) and calls us to behave ourselves in a manner consistent with such a definition.

I Will Build My Church

I will build my church- The church is Jesus Church and Jesus is the builder. The church is not built by man (human) not by programs or methods. Jesus purchases this church with his blood Christ is the rock upon which the church is built. The church is built by him, on him and for him. It is for him that he builds his church he gives the keys of binding and loosing. If two or three are gathered together in my name he is in the mist of them. Jesus is in agreement with his bride (church).

Jesus set up his bride that will bring and birth spiritual children to her husband and as the bride of Christ we are to bring forth fruits (children of righteousness to have fellowship with God, we must begin with God and his authoritative Revelation of himself (word).

(Holiness) God is light in him there is no darkness at all

John 3:19 (KJV)

19 And this is the condemnation, that light is come into the world, and men loved darkness rather than light, because their deeds were evil.

If you don't begin with God's holiness, you will never understand God's plan of salvation through the cross.

Prophetic intercessors is the main function of a prophet is not to predict and speak nice words of personal prophesy over people and tell them what their life purpose is going to be and who they're going to get married, and whether they're going to be rich. People read horoscope for that Satan does that. That is not the work of the prophetic ministry.

House of Prayer

As we look to the early church the church was a praying church. The Lord told his disciple to always pray when God visit he comes to stay. He is not interested only in visitations but also habitation. He wants a place to dwell (live) Jesus said; my father house shall be called a house of prayer.

Matthew 6:5 (KJV)

5 And when thou pray, thou shall not be as the hypocrites are: for they love to pray standing in the synagogues and the corners of the streets, that they may be seen of men. Verily I say unto you, they have their reward.

When we pray in secret and come together in the open to the house of God where two or three gather together in his name (Jesus) supernatural begin to take place.

2nd Chronicles 7:14 (KJV)

14 If my people, which are called by my name, shall humble themselves, and pray, and seek my face (presence), and turn from their wicked ways; then will I hear from heaven, and will forgive their sin, and will heal their land.

Praying is what we all should do be doing if we are born again believers prayer is talking to God. Jesus was angry with the Priest and Scribes, and Pharisees for selling in the temple. I call it money changers, while they were selling instead of praying in the temple the House of God.

Jesus made it very clear that if we want to succeed in ministry we must pray above all things. This is what happen at rebirth when you were born again God transfer you out of darkness (Satan kingdom, the world) into his marvelous light his kingdom. Jesus traded places with you he now lives in you to grow, and mature to continue his work for the kingdom of Heaven "He said greater works we will do". We have the power and authority to cast out devils, heal the sick, and speak with new tongues.

We are to teach all nations, make disciples of others and grow in Christ learn who we are in him and bring other into the kingdom and teach them the cycle continue as they grow learning and teaching. Prayer is our foundation to all that we learn and do.

Matthew 28:19-20 (KJV)

19 Go you therefore, and teach all nations, baptizing them in the name of the Father, and of the Son, and of the Holy Ghost:

20 Teaching them to observe all things whatsoever I have commanded you: and lo, I am with you always, even unto the end of the world. Amen.

From Religion to a Revelation

After we have gone through all of the religious ceremonies, dancing, shouting, running, screaming, jumping all of our religious form of Godliness and denying the power. Then we come into the true knowledge of Jesus Christ starting a true relationship with him. Coming through our wilderness of dry land and let Christ be formed in us. Having a true relationship with him will change everything you believe you were taught; you learned and did not learn.

This is important to truly have a relationship with Jesus. How will we teach all nations to be disciples when we have not yet been disciples unto Christ? I have found that religion with really mess people up so bad that they are deceived into believing anything just because there is no teacher to teach.

Not everyone that say unto me Lord, Lord, shall enter into the kingdom of heaven, but he that doeth the will of my father which is in heaven many wonderful work? And I will profess unto you; depart from me, ye that work iniquity.

Jesus said I do know you because you never took the time to know me to develop a relationship with you. I never had the privilege to teach you to train you be intimate with you. You were too busy working for man and not God we need to develop a relationship with him so he can teach us so we can teach others.

Revelation: The Church Needs a Facelift

We are told of God to get back to the old land mark. If we continue to play church things will get worst not only for the people of God, but also for the world. We are called out to make a difference the church is the only system that will make a difference in this ungodly contaminated world.

Apart From Me

We cannot have the gifts in operation without the fruits of the Spirit for they are in harmony with each other Jesus said; apart from me you can do nothing. One of the primary purposes of the Holy Spirit in our life (the believers) life is to transform us to the image of Christ to make us more and more like Jesus in every aspect in our life. Our sinful nature is in contest with God.

Galatians 5:19-21 (KJV)

19 Now the works of the flesh are these: Adultery, fornication, uncleanness, lasciviousness,

20 Idolatry, witchcraft, hatred, variance, emulations, wrath, strife, seditions, heresies,

21 Envying, murders, drunkenness, retellings, and such like: of these which I tell you before, as I have also told you in time past, that they which do such things shall not inherit the kingdom of God.

These are not the fruits that the Holy Spirit produces in the life of the believers. Jesus did not go around doing these he was a man in the flesh who lived a Holy life unto God his father. Even after we are born again the spiritual life is still a battle.

The flesh is at war with the spirit man this is why it is important so important to receive the gift of the Holy Spirit, because it is the Holy Spirit job to produce the fruits of the spirit in our lives. In order to be victorious and live in victory this is how God desires for his children to live a victorious life in Christ.

John 15:1-4 (KJV)

1 I am the true vine, and my Father is the husbandman.

2 Every branch in me that bear not fruit he takes away: and every branch that bear fruit, he purge it, that it may bring

forth more fruit.

3 Now ye are clean through the word which I have spoken unto you.

4 Abide in me, and I in you. As the branch cannot bear fruit of itself, except it abide in the vine; no more can ye, except ye abide in me.

True followers of Christ will be recognized by their fruit. First the fruits we beat in our personal life then the fruits we bear outwardly. We are (you are) to be made into the image of Christ.

(1) Love- John 15:13 (KJV)

Greater love hath no man than this that a man lay down his life for his friends.

(2) Joy- The joy of the Lord is our strength his joy that fills us is unspeakable, we sing the song I have joy when I think about what he done for me.

(3) Peace- Isaiah 26:3

Thou wilt keep him in perfect peace, whose mind is stayed on thee: because he trusted in thee.

He who mind stays on him he will keep them in prefect peace, because he trusts in you. There is not any comparing with the peace of God. I remember when I first was saved peace was all around me, even my children were at peace oh! What peace it was.

(4) Patience God's patience leads us to repentance longsuffering with others. Slow to anger this stronghold has its disadvantage anger rage, short temper, unable to wait on something or someone. But let patient have her perfect work. I admit this one is/was one of my stumbling blocks in my life. I thank and praise God for his grace and mercy toward me.

(5) Kindness it really pays to be kind to others, but what do we do when we are kind to others and they are against us or take our kindness as a sign of weakness? Without the spirit it is hard to be kind to these types of people we struggle saying I try to be kind to her/him. But I am not going to be any longer. The word tells us to be kind to each other and exalt each other daily.

(6) Goodness I use to get kindness and goodness mixed up I would say, what is the difference? Goodness is being unselfish, doing an act of sacrifice. James 1:17 (KJV) Every good and perfect gift comes from above only by his spirit can unselfishness be removed.

(7) Faithfulness believing that God is who he says he is and not be moved by any lies, trickery, craftiness or schemes of people and the enemy. Believe God's promises steadfastness unmovable. The Holy Spirit will witness to our spirit the God of the bible, his promises, word and our inheritance in him.

When I first came to Christ is was hard for me to believe God was a God who did what he said he would do in the bible. He had to take me through some lows and some highs: He had to strength my faith. What was awesome and amazing to me is when he spoke directly to my spirit. WOW! All I could say was I heard you Lord let him do it for you and he will.

Gentleness-The Holy Spirit is a gentleman he is gentle, meek, sometimes he is humorous, has a sense of humor, polite, humility. Whenever I meet someone with a gentle spirit I can tell right away it is the work of the Holy Spirit in their life.

Galatians 6:1 (KJV)

1 Brethren, if a man be overtaken in a fault, ye which are

spiritual, restore such a one in the spirit of meekness; considering thyself, lest thou also be tempted.

Self-control the ability to control yourself. We are no longer "slave to sin".

Romans 6:6 (KJV)

6 Knowing this, that our old man is crucified with him, that the body of sin might be destroyed, that henceforth we should not serve sin.

God has separated his people from worldly people if we continue to hang around people who don't believe in the God of heaven then we are putting ourselves in a position to be attacked by ungodly people who make fun of God who is Holy and call us to be Holy.

What kind of friendship can a believer have with an unbeliever? Bad company corrupts good character.

Chapter 17

Prophecy

He makes His Ministers Flames of Fire

The Lord says: I am igniting my ministers as flames of fire to release my anointing to this generation. They will come in my power and my authority and they will be a blaze with my glory. I will send them out to rekindle the flames that have died out and rekindle the embers that have been left smoldering in the lives of those who have lost their zeal.

I am rekindling the fire of those in the fivefold ministry and releasing them back into their position. I am rekindling the fire of those who were once used in spiritual gifts who have become weary and lost their passion.

I am rekindling the fire of those in the fivefold ministry and releasing them back into their position. I am rekindling the fire of those who were once used in spiritual gifts who have become weary and lost their passion.

I am rekindling the fire to those who are called to go out and set the world ablaze. I will send my winds and breathe my pneumatic, as I fan the flames and bring fire back into your lives and ministries.

Now is the time for my glory to be radiant throughout the land. What seemed charred, seared and stagnant in your life will be revived as my fire ignites a new passion in your soul. I will send my fire across this nation and around this world and I am looking for those who will release my glory for such a time as this.

They are those who are willing to lay down their lives and tale ups their cross. They are those who have counted the cost and aligned their lives to my agenda will be used mightily in my end time army.

They are those who will not allow the enemy to quench this fire or rattle their faith. They are those who will be set ablaze to go forth to fan the flames and stroke fires in others.

They will go forth and do great exploits they will stir themselves up and renew the passion that others once had in their hearts.

As you take the limits off me you will experience a fire that you have not known before. Don't settle for a mediocre lifestyle but receive all that I have for you.

Now my word to penetrate your heart as a fire shut up in your bones as you see a shifting and shaking in the natural realm, knows that there is also spiritual shifting.

There is unseen activity happening simultaneously in the heavenliest. Just as there are fires in the natural, I am sending a spiritual fire that the enemy will not be able to extinguish.

Angelic activity is being released from the third heaven that no man or demon can quench. Do not fears the days ahead but know that I am releasing my glory in a magnitude which no human or devil could stop says the Lord.

Hebrew 1:7 (KJV)

"In speaking of angels he says, and of the angels he said, who make his angels spirits, and his ministers a Flame of Fire."

What Is a Bride?

/bird/ Noun

A woman on her wedding day or just before or after the event.

Synonyms: wife marriage partner, newlywed

Robert's lovely wife (bride}

A bride is a woman about to be married or newlywed.

If one is a born again believer washed in his blood, bought/purchased, redeemed by his blood you are a bride being prepared for her husband the bride of Christ.

He is coming back for a bride without spot, wrinkles or blemishes. That is why the sanctification process is so important so his bride can be cleansed by the washing of the water of the word.

Revelation 21:2 (KJV)

2 And I John saw the holy city, New Jerusalem, coming down from God out of heaven, prepared as a bride adorned for her husband.

The Bride of Christ

Ephesians 5:25-26 (KJV)

25 Husband, love your wives, even as Christ also loved the church, and gave himself for it.

26 That he might present it to himself a glorious church, not having spot, or wrinkle, of any such thing; but that it should be holy and without blemish.

Jesus loves his church and sacrificed his own life for her he sanctifies and cleanses the church (bride) through his word.

Revelation 21:9 (KJV)

9 And there came unto me one of the seven angels which had the seven vials full of the seven last plagues, and talked with me, saying, Come hither, I will show thee the bride, the Lamb's wife.

As a bride one has to allow the Lord to take you through the sanctification process. The process is not easy, because God has to put to death the things of the flesh.

The New Jerusalem, the city of God coming down from heaven. The church is the bride of the Lamb, the Lamb who takes away the sin of the world, who judges in righteousness as a lion, lives with his people forever.

The church (bride) is the true church of God his people who trust in him. A picture of the church is we can look in the book of Acts once again.

Acts 2:42-47 (KJV)

42 And they continued steadfastly in the apostles' doctrine and fellowship, and in breaking of bread, and in prayers.

43 And fear came upon every soul: and many wonders and signs were done by the apostles.

44 And all that believed were together, and had all things common;

45 And sold their possessions and goods, and parted them to all men, as every man had need.

46 And they, continuing daily with one accord in the temple, and breaking bread from house to house, did eat their meat with gladness and singleness of heart,

47 Praising God and having favor with all the people. And the Lord added to the church daily such as should be saved.

The church focus was on discipleship as we know no church

is perfect, but the government order should be as God pattern his people to be and do.

We are no longer witnessing because we are too busy trying to get stuff. Jesus said where your heart is there your treasure is also. Through dreams and visions God is leading his bride.

At War

The truth is we are at war our enemy is Satan, we are to be trained how to fight and overcome the enemy, learn his tactic, his stagey, his lies, his deceptions our mind is the battlefield (battleground). Our weapons of our warfare are not (worldly) but they are mighty through God for the pulling down of strongholds pulling down every imagination that exalts itself against the knowledge of God and bring every thought captive to the obedience of Christ. For the believer our daily battleground is the progressive state of renewing our minds.

How Do We Renew Our Minds?

We study; read, mediate on the word of God daily and night every chance we get only then we can wage a good warfare. This is the process of spiritual transformation, study.

Joshua 1:8 (KJV)

8 This book of the law shall not depart out of thy mouth; but thou shall meditate therein day and night, that thou may observe to do according to all that is written therein: for then thou shall make thy way prosperous, and then thou shall have good success.

Salvation Prayer

Dear God in heaven, I come to you in the name of Jesus. I acknowledge to you that I am a sinner, and I am sorry for my sins and the life that I have lived I ask that you forgive me. I believe that your only begotten son Jesus Christ shed his precious blood on the cross at Calvary and died for my sins, and I am now willing to turn from my sins thank you for forgiving me.

Romans 10:9 (KJV)

9 That if thou shall confess with thy mouth the Lord Jesus, and shall believe in thy heart that God hath raised him from the dead, thou shall be saved.

Dying to Self

Our Lord and savior died and shed his blood on the cross at Calvary. He died for his church (bride) and purchased it with his own blood. Jesus died so that his born again may live dying to self will be an exchange with him. Jesus exchanged life with his believers as he has died so does his blood washed must die to self so that he can live his life through them.

When you re purposely set aside, rejected, forgotten, and hurt with the insult of oversight- but your spirit sings because you are being counted worthy to suffer for Christ we call it "Dying to Self." When all manner of evil is spoken against you, and you refuse to let it get the best of you.

Dying to self when you keep silent and not fight back, take accusation, be patient do not be ignorant, prideful, selfish and you keep your peace as Jesus endured it is call dying to self.

Romans 6:11 (KJV)

11 Likewise reckon you also yourselves to be dead indeed unto sin, but alive unto God through Jesus Christ our Lord.

Dying to self which involves making choices like dying to our ways and living unto the Lord's ways. The power of man's will make him overcome or send him to tell his people body (flesh) in order to live. If we follow the example of the Good Shepherd take up our cross and follow him daily we will do well in the sight of our Lord.

Trusting in his word by faith walking like he walked pray like he prayed. He shed his blood so that his bride will accomplish the work for her to carry on until his return. He paid the price for the sins of all mankind.

Hebrews 9:22 (KJV)

22 And almost all things are be the law purged with blood; and without shedding of blood is no remission (forgiveness).

The Blood of Jesus

(1) Cleanses

(2) We have life in his blood

(3) Gives health and strength

(4) His blood feeds us

(5) His blood protects

Purchase by his own blood, redeemed from the curse of the law being made a curse for us gave his life and after all of that he calls us his friend. What more can we ask for? What else is there to do? He has done it all!

Now he will return for his bride for the choice is ours to choose life or death. Jesus is the last and ultimate sacrifice.

Acts 20:28 (KJV)

28 Take heed therefore unto yourselves, and to all the flock, over that which the Holy Ghost hath made you overseers,

to feed the church of God, which he hath purchased with his own blood.

Cleanses

Ephesians 5:25-27 (KJV)

25 Husband, love your wives, even as Christ also loved the church, and gave himself for it;

26 That he might sanctify and cleanse it with the washing of water by the word,

27 That he might present it to himself a glorious church, not having spot, or wrinkle, or any such thing; but that it should be holy and without blemish.

Life in the Blood

Jesus said; "I am the bread of life giving up our former way of life to follow him." It is an inside out job the change begins on the inside of us bringing about a change in us from glory to glory. The bread of life is the word of God, Jesus is the word the spoken word God reveals to us in simple form that we may come to know God when we hear the word who is Jesus and accept the word into our minds, our hearts, our spirit and let the word begin to change us. Every step of the way to God will be through Jesus the bread of life. This bread feed our spirit life; feed our soul, not our bodies.

Christian Dreams Interpretation

Just a little touch about the dreams and vision symbols, Christian dream interpretation is vital and must be spirit led. We must learn to know and understand what the Lord is saying to us in dreams and visions. He speaks to us in dark saying to keep his will secret and hidden from the enemy.

Not every symbol has the same interpretation for every person. What a spouse or a father in one person's dream may represent something totally different in another. So as a prophet in addition to using these guidelines, ask the Lord for revelation to add to the dream while going through the dream, write out the interpretation by journaling and allow the Holy Spirit to place additional pictures and revelation into your heart to enhance it.

Dreams can tell you all about a person it can let you know what is in their heart and what the Lord is doing in their lives.

Use the opportunity, not just give a dream interpretation but also for ministry. This is after all what the Lord gives revelation for, for ministry and encouragement. Take the interpretation the Lord gives you and then add encouragement and counseling to give the person faith, hope and love. As you use the gifts within you, you will be a sharpened, valuable tool in the hand of the master and treasure in his eyes.

Background Information

We want to interpret by the spirit and the word.

Symbols also depend on your culture and upbringing.

Are you struggling with understanding the prophetic and prophesy in the bible?

Are you struggling with understanding your gifts, identity in the body of Christ?

Are you ready to know who you are in him the purpose for your calling in the kingdom of God?

Operating under the anointing and the prophetic is part of the Kingdom.

(1). Walking in the prophetic which comes from the third realm of the third heaven

(2). God wants you to know your true identity in the in Christ and in the body of Christ.

(3). Applying the basic biblical principle to your life following the patriarchs in the old and new testament who walked and demonstrated the power and obedience of God. It is time to come out of religious ceremonies and walk in true freedom of Christ. Jesus gave the church his authority and power to do the work of the kingdom. His body of believers is to bring the Kingdom of God into alignment. We are to make disciples of all nations. Dreams and Visions are part of the kingdom of God they are a mystery until now. God secrets are being uncovered as we grow up in him.

In this book there is not much explanation of the dreams and visions. I have written another book for the interpretation of the dreams and visions. I would like to uncover and give revelations on this subject. God wants everyone to come into the revelation knowledge of their dreams and what they mean also how God speaks in them concern your life, where we are in him spiritually. This is my passion after God begin to reveal to me his will through dreams concerning my life. I do want to say just as other gifts he does not want us to be lead completely by them and get into error. God does not want us to make our dreams our gods. I have had people that wanted interpretation, but do not study the word of God his word should be first, because our dreams are to line up with his word. This book is mostly word based, meaning based on Gods' word. I am excited about this revelation is continually receiving revelation about dreams and vision. This word may not be for you some books that I read do not agree with my spirit, but if you are confused and interested in your dreams and vision have been asking what they mean? How do I understand these dreams? I dream all the time never know what they mean than this book is for you. My book on the interpretations is more in detail.

www.ingramcontent.com/pod-product-compliance
Lightning Source LLC
Chambersburg PA
CBHW071456070526
44578CB00001B/368